Expert Adjustments of Model Forecasts

To what extent should anybody who has to make model forecasts generated from detailed data analysis adjust their forecasts based on their own intuition? In this book, Philip Hans Franses, one of Europe's leading econometricians, presents the notion that many publicly available forecasts have experienced an 'expert's touch', and questions whether this type of intervention is useful and if a lighter adjustment would be more beneficial. Covering an extensive research area, this accessible book brings together current theoretical insights and new empirical results to examine expert adjustment from an econometric perspective. The author's analysis is based on a range of real forecasts and the datasets upon which the forecasters relied. The various motivations behind experts' modifications are considered, and guidelines for creating more useful and reliable adjusted forecasts are suggested. This book will appeal to academics and practitioners with an interest in forecasting methodology.

PHILIP HANS FRANSES is Professor of Applied Econometrics and Professor of Marketing Research at the Erasmus University Rotterdam. Since 2006 he has served as the Dean of the Erasmus School of Economics. His research interests concern the development and application of econometric methods for problems in marketing, finance and macroeconomics.

Expert Adjustments of Model Forecasts

Theory, Practice and Strategies for Improvement

PHILIP HANS FRANSES

CAMBRIDGE
UNIVERSITY PRESS

CAMBRIDGE
UNIVERSITY PRESS

University Printing House, Cambridge CB2 8BS, United Kingdom

Cambridge University Press is part of the University of Cambridge.

It furthers the University's mission by disseminating knowledge in the pursuit of education, learning and research at the highest international levels of excellence.

www.cambridge.org
Information on this title: www.cambridge.org/9781107081598

First published 2014

A catalogue record for this publication is available from the British Library

Library of Congress Cataloguing in Publication data
Franses, Philip Hans, 1963–
Expert adjustments of model forecasts : theory, practice and strategies for improvement / Philip Hans Franses.
   pages   cm
ISBN 978-1-107-08159-8 (hardback)
1. Econometric models.   2. Economic forecasting.   3. Business
forecasting.   I. Title.
HB141.F69   2014
330.01'12–dc23

                                          2014021767

ISBN 978-1-107-08159-8 Hardback
ISBN 978-1-107-44161-3 Paperback

'We are all aliens to ourselves,
and if we have any sense of who we are,
it is only because we live inside the eyes of others.'
(Auster, 2012)

Contents

Figures

Tables

Preface

This monograph aims to collect together recent theoretical insights and various empirical results for a rapidly developing area concerning the analysis of business and economic forecasts. Strictly following econometric textbooks, it is tempting to assume that forecasts are the result of a careful modelling exercise, and that the econometric model-builder delivers the forecast to an end-user. However, since the mid 1980s the literature has contained various studies which suggest that the model-builder is not always the last person to deal with the forecast, and there can be someone in between the model-builder and the end-user, whom I will call the expert. This expert can modify or adjust the model forecast, after having received it and evaluated it, and it is this adjusted forecast which is typically delivered to the end-user. The early literature contains some scattered examples where such an adjustment occurs, sometimes to the benefit of the quality of the forecast, but sometimes not. Recent literature shows a revived interest in these expert-adjusted forecasts, for various reasons. First, and as will be argued in this book, it turns out that many, if perhaps not all, economic forecasts seem to undergo some tweaking from an expert. The recent availability of very large databases with expert-adjusted forecasts and model forecasts emphasizes this outcome. Second, there is a revived interest in analysing the quality of economic forecasts, and when experts have adjusted econometric model forecasts it may be necessary to rethink how such final forecasts should be evaluated. Third, it will be interesting to understand what it is that an expert does, in particular in cases where they themselves do not say. Below we will see that there are many possible reasons for experts to modify forecasts, and in this book I aim to put the experts' behaviour into an econometric perspective. I will argue that adjusting model forecasts can be quite a good idea, and there are some potentially useful guidelines. It is hoped that this book will rouse the interest of academics and practitioners to pursue further research and obtain practical experience in order to learn how to create useful and reliable forecasts.

My interest in this area basically started with the analysis of a large database that I was able to acquire from a large pharmaceutical company. So, in addition to an overview of the earlier studies in the forecasting literature and more recent accounts, this book also covers most of my findings and insights in a single volume. My research has been spurred by the availability of various very valuable databases, which I (of course with the help of students and colleagues) was allowed to analyse. Based on these analyses, theories were developed, and with these we were able to make recommendations to practitioners. Most of our results have been published in articles in international journals, which I will not replicate, although I will highlight the outcomes. The chronology of my articles on this topic shows how our insights were obtained, and in which order. However, with hindsight this chronology should be different, and in fact, if the reader were to read my research work in chronological order, it would be quite easy to lose the main insights. Hence, I decided to write this book to put all my results into a proper sequential perspective.

It all began with a lecture that I gave in 2006 in Brussels. In 2004 I had published an article in *Interfaces* entitled 'Do we think we make better forecasts than in the past? A survey of academics' (Franses, 2004). One of the conclusions of the survey was that half the interviewed academics believed that econometric or statistical model forecasts could be improved by (somehow) including the domain knowledge of experts. Until that moment, I had rarely considered this notion, because as a trained econometrician I had always believed that forecasting only from econometric models was always the best option. Sometime in 2005, I was approached by people from a company called Marcus Evans, who were looking for a speaker at a conference to be organized in Brussels, on 16 and 17 March 2006, with the theme 'Making supply meet demand'. In the midst of hectic times in our Erasmus School of

Economics, I thought it would be nice to do something different, and I accepted the invitation. My presentation, accordingly entitled 'Forecasting demand, can we do better these days?', was scheduled right before lunch on 16 March. The last slide mentioned that 'models may benefit from expert adjustment', but, I concluded, 'how to add such knowledge and how to evaluate adjusted forecasts is still an open question'. I was invited to join the lunch and at the table was a fellow Dutchman, who introduced himself as Sander Demouge from the Netherlands-based pharmaceutical company Organon. He said, 'We have the same problem at Organon where we have data on forecasts from experts and from an automated forecast support system (FSS), and we want to know how to interpret those expert forecasts. Can we perhaps talk to you one day to see if together we can find a way out?' My 'Yes, of course, with pleasure' marked the start of the research project, various highlights of which are now summarized in this book.

Sander and I met again in November 2006 when he presented the issues at stake at Organon. They had a version of ForecastPro™ – forecasting software, which they used to generate statistical model-based sales forecasts each month for all their products sold in forty-plus countries. At the same time, local managers quoted their own forecasts, and these were also recorded and stored. Organon's key problem was that they had announced bonus payments for these managers depending on how much more accurate their forecasts were compared to the statistical model, but the company did not know how to measure that quality effectively. I said that I was more than happy to help, and if I did, would Organon allow me and my team to publish the outcomes if these were of enough interest to international publications? A few days later Sander confirmed that publishing was no problem as long as we did not mention the product names and the countries. On 20 December 2006 I received the spreadsheet with the data, and this file turned out to be huge. In modern-day language one would call this database an example of 'big data'. It contained all the information that was needed to analyse the differences between model forecasts and expert forecasts, for hundreds of products, sold in various months from 2004 to 2006 in a range of countries on all continents for horizons one month to twenty-four months. This was an amazing database, and I could not wait to start the analysis. One nice feature of it was that I also received data on some of the traits of the managers (experts) who were responsible for making the forecasts.

In September 2006 I started as the Dean of the Erasmus School of Economics, and this hampered me from making a quick start on analysing Organon's database. To be honest, my complete lack of skills with programs such as Excel, in which the data were presented, also did not help progress. Luckily I was able to hire Rianne Legerstee, one of the most gifted students ever to attend our Econometric Institute. She spent almost the first six months of 2007 sorting the data so that they could be analysed. This meticulous work turned out to be extremely useful, as we could put together various papers. We wrote various reports for Organon and in the autumn of 2007 we presented our results, which Organon also shared with their managers during a training session. They were very happy with our results, which among other things showed that the expert forecasts were rarely better than the model forecasts. So they now also had a reason to stop linking forecast performance with bonuses. The training session turned out to be very helpful, as we demonstrated in a 2011 report and a 2014 paper (summarized in Chapter 5 below). In January 2008, Organon was taken over by an American company, and a little later Sander Demouge informed me that he had moved to another job.

Rianne and I kept working on these data, and we tried to publish our results in international academic journals. This turned out not to be immediately very successful, and it was not until early 2009 that we had our first piece accepted. In 2008 Rianne accepted my offer to study for a PhD, and in 2012 she graduated with a thesis that included two papers that also dealt with the Organon data. It is fair to say that without Rianne Legerstee there would have been no papers, without Sander Demouge there would have been no data, and without my lecture in Brussels, there would have been no book.

In the meantime I got more and more involved in the topic of the interaction between experts and models, and this led to contacts with

KLM Royal Dutch Airlines, the Netherlands Bureau of Economic Policy Analysis (CPB) and Bayer in Leverkusen, Germany. I was allowed to analyse expert forecasts and model forecasts (if they were available). I thank Pieter Bootsma and Stefan ten Haaf of KLM, Henk Kranendonk and Debby Lanser of CPB, and Prasad Saraph, Christopher Baron and Achim Siegert of Bayer for their generous help with their data. Amazingly, Henk and Debby of the CPB were so kind as to re-create the CPB model forecasts using the older versions of the model, which turned out to be an enormous effort.

The Econometric Institute of the Erasmus School of Economics is by far the best place in the world to work as an econometrician. It hosts the best students, and I would specifically like to mention Bert de Bruijn and Marjolein van Baardwijk for their assistance. The institute also hosts the best colleagues, and here I would like to thank Richard Paap, Dennis Fok, Dick van Dijk, Patrick Groenen, Christiaan Heij, Michael McAleer, Michel van der Velden and Alex Koning for their helpful suggestions over the years, and for their co-authorship on various projects, including some referred to in this book.

I am very proud that this book will be incorporated in the catalogue of Cambridge University Press. It is a great honour to me that they want to publish this book, and I am very thankful to my editor Chris Harrison for his ongoing trust in my academic endeavours. Also, four anonymous reviewers gave detailed and very helpful suggestions, which seriously improved this book. Parts of the book were presented as lectures at the Econometric Institute of the Erasmus School of Economics, the Netherlands Bureau for Economic Policy Analysis (CPB), Organon, the University of Groningen, and at the International Symposia on Forecasting in 2011 (Prague) and 2013 (Seoul).

To end this preface, I would like to dedicate this book to two individuals who have been very important to me and my career. The first is my PhD supervisor Teun Kloek. When I finished my PhD thesis in 1991 I had learned that econometrics was the best academic subject there is, and that, basically, everything is interesting to study. The second is my incomparable senior colleague Clive Granger who unfortunately died way too early. In 2007, when we were enjoying the sea winds around Neeltje Jans, he asked me 'Why would someone like you be so stupid as to become a Dean?' I replied that I hoped to have enough time to do some research, and with this book I hope that I would have convinced him that I did.

Anyway, the main lesson that I can give to anyone who reads this book is that if you are asked to give a lecture, do it, and also pose a few questions to the audience: you never know what will happen.

1 Introduction

This monograph deals with the situation where an analyst evaluates expert forecasts and model forecasts, and where it is known that the expert has seen the model forecast and thus that the expert forecast potentially amounts to an adjustment of the model forecast. More precisely, the analyst assumes that

$$\text{Expert-Adjusted Forecast} = \alpha \text{ times Model Forecast}$$
$$+ \text{ Adjustment.} \qquad (1.1)$$

This additive expression is chosen for analytical convenience, as will become clear in Chapter 2, and also to easily allow for the possibility that the model forecast and the expert forecast have opposite signs.

It is important to stress that the analyst only observes the model forecast and the final expert forecast, and of course also the realized observation, but that the analyst does not observe the value of α, nor the size of the adjustment. In many practical settings, the analyst is usually not the same individual as the expert who adjusts the model forecast, nor is the analyst the same person as the model-builder. In fact, the analyst may have to report to management or to policymakers on the usefulness and relevance of the final expert forecasts, perhaps relative to the model forecast. Such expert forecasts can concern business and economic variables: for example, sales of durable products, earnings of companies or macroeconomic variables like gross domestic product (GDP) or inflation. The forecasts may have to be generated very frequently, for example, hourly, or they may also be quoted just once every half-year.

There is one particular feature that is very important here and that is that the experts are assumed to quote their forecasts *given* that they have received model-based forecasts. It is, however, uncertain if

1

and how they actually incorporate the model forecasts into their decision process, as usually there is no written documentation. So it may be that an expert sets α equal to 0, and fully bases the final expert forecast on his or her own judgement, but this is unknown to the analyst. Indeed, typically, experts do not document how they decide on the values of α and the adjustment.

It is irrelevant whether the model forecasts originate from multi-equation macroeconomic models or from simple extrapolation tools, or anything in between. It may very well be that an expert does not know what the model or forecast algorithm looks like, and in most practical cases it also holds that the expert cannot exercise any influence on how the model forecasts are created. It is usually the case that the expert is not the same person who designs the model, but no specific assumptions on this feature have to be made. The models and their parameters can be updated every single hour, or they may be taken as constant for a long period of time. The statistical tools with which the models are calibrated are largely irrelevant, and it may well be that the expert in fact does not have a clear-cut idea of how the model forecasts were created. In the end, the situation is that the analyst observes an expert forecast, a model forecast and a realization, and the analyst has to evaluate the expert forecast using some criterion.

A key premise of the analysis in this book is that the analyst does not know α or the size of the adjustment and that the analyst is also unaware of *how* the expert has chosen a value of α and the adjustment. The size of these two features, that is, α, and the adjustment, can be set by the expert using his or her own intuition or model, but how that is done is usually unknown. The definition of 'intuition' is obtained from the *Oxford Dictionary* and is 'the ability to understand something instinctively, without the need for conscious reasoning'. At the same time, it may also be that the expert uses knowledge that can be documented and evaluated. For example, a known future regime shift may not be incorporated in the model and thus not in the model forecast, and the expert may use this knowledge to assign a value to the adjustment.

It seems easiest to presume that the expert is a single individual who makes his or her own decisions, but it cannot be excluded that the empirical cases to be analysed below concern cases where a group of experts have jointly decided on α and the adjustment. It can happen that forecasts are adjusted during a group meeting, and that perhaps colleagues interfere, but that is usually unknown in many practical settings. Indeed, if expert forecasts are the outcome of a group process, then all sorts of potential biases may occur, but these are not addressed in this book.

As I have said, it is assumed that the expert is not the same person as the one who is responsible for the model forecast. In other words, experts are assumed to modify a final model forecast, and not particular elements of the econometric model or the statistical algorithm. Of course, model-builders also use their judgement to create their model and subsequent model forecasts, and in the modelling process they can make the adjustments to intercepts, parameters for important variables, and, for example, recent values of explanatory variables. Indeed, much judgement is usually also involved when building a model. One needs to select variables, choose model selection criteria, think of the choice of measurement, and perhaps rely on summarizing techniques like principal components analysis (PCA). One may also have to choose between various parameter estimation methods. All these aspects are assumed to be incorporated in the model forecast that arrives on the expert's desk. So, it is the judgement of the expert that is at stake here, and not the decisions of the model-builder.

A further important premise in this book is that the analyst actually observes the model forecast. Naturally, this facilitates the evaluation of the expert forecasts. This is not always the case, however. Think of the forecasts generated by the IMF, the OECD or the World Bank, where the underlying model is not usually presented, nor are the associated model forecasts (if there are any) displayed in their reports. From an econometric perspective, this lack of available model forecasts can be accommodated by assuming that the analyst has his or her own econometric skills and can create a model using the information available. That is, the analyst can somehow approximate the unavailable model forecasts by designing his or her own econometric model based on publicly available data, and use these as the pseudo-model forecasts, but again that can only be viewed as an approximation. As will become clear in later chapters, these approximations can also be quite informative when evaluating final expert forecasts that could have been based on model forecasts.

Another important stance in this book is that the analyst can only sensibly evaluate the expert-adjusted forecasts if the analyst can approximate what the expert did when he or she received the model forecasts. In other words, to properly analyse the usefulness and accuracy of the final expert forecasts, the analyst somehow needs to infer values for α and the adjustment. Indeed, experts may decide to fully incorporate the model forecasts (meaning that they set α at 1) and just add or subtract a little bit, but they may also wholly ignore the input from an econometric model or statistical algorithm altogether (meaning that they set α at 0). As will be argued in Chapter 2, it will be quite relevant to approximate what the expert does in order to properly evaluate the forecasts. That same chapter will indicate the optimal values of α and the adjustment to make the expert-adjusted forecasts most useful, at least from an econometric perspective.

In a nutshell, the critical questions in this book are the following. If it is assumed that:

Expert-Adjusted Forecast = α times Model Forecast
+ Adjustment,

what then are the optimal values and properties of α and the adjustment, at least from an econometric perspective? As will become clear from Chapter 2, among other insights, is that the adjustment can be large or small: that is, the size of the adjustment does not matter, at least in theory, but the adjustment better not be based on the same information that is used to create the model forecast. The next question is, given the optimality results, how close to the optimal setting are empirical values of α and the adjustment in a range of actual practical cases? And when prevailing practice does not match theoretical optimality, as it seems not to do, how does this effect forecast accuracy? Finally, if there seems to be a gap between theory and practice and it does hurt accuracy, are there any sensible strategies for improvement?

INSIGHTS FROM THE LITERATURE ON DECISION-MAKING

Before the focus in this book becomes an econometric one, it seems relevant to consult the literature on decision-making to learn about potential insights concerning α and the adjustment. The decision-making literature is very large and is still growing, but much of the relevant material for the present book is summarized in Kahneman's *Thinking, Fast and Slow* (2012).

One angle on forecasting could be that the expert forecast is not based on a model or algorithm, but that it holds true that

Expert Forecast = Intuition.

In the first part of Kahneman (2012) it is convincingly argued that when forecasts are based not on statistical algorithms but only on intuition, it is quite likely that all kinds of biases are in play, and that these biases negatively impact on forecast accuracy. For example, individuals have a tendency to ignore the phenomenon called 'regression to the mean', which entails that when exceptional events occurred, say, yesterday, it is quite likely that such events will not occur again today. In fact and in contrast, individuals seem ready to believe that recent exceptional events mark the start of a series of such events, and hence a trend will be spotted where there effectively is no such trend. The fact that there is a focus on only a single exceptional event also masks the notion that other events could have occurred too, and that basically the sample size is equal to 1. In his Chapter 18, Kahneman (2012) thus argues that intuition-based forecasts are often based on too much confidence and are often too extreme, and that they ignore the regression-to-the-mean tendency (see also Shanteau, 1992). Building on the influential work of Taleb (2007), who addresses the bias called 'the illusion of understanding', individuals have a tendency to be confident in their interpretation of past events, and they seem to ignore the fact that matters could have been different. Additionally, due to hindsight bias, individuals also have difficulties in reconstructing how they relied on their intuition the last time they created a forecast.

The various biases that can hamper the quality of expert forecasts are convincingly illustrated in the analysis of Tetlock (2005). Political forecasts created by experts turned out not to be so good, and the suggestion is therefore that: 'Another reason for the inferiority of expert judgement is that humans are incorrigibly inconsistent in making summary judgements of complex information' (Kahneman, 2012: 224). Hence, it does not seem wise to ignore a model forecast, if indeed there is one, in favour of a forecast based wholly on the intuition of an expert. Dawes (1979) recommends the use of simple algorithms instead of complicated regression models, but, as mentioned, for the experts adjusting model forecasts the type of model is not very important. And Simon (1992) proposes relying on intuition when it is based on pattern recognition – that is, a set of rules that can be understood and replicated – and this recommendation comes close to what will be reported in Chapter 2 below. That is, the values of α and the adjustment should best be based on the replicable knowledge of an expert.

Kahneman (2012) also convincingly argues in favour of relying on a model or algorithm: 'Because you have little direct knowledge of what goes on in your mind, you will never know that you might have made a different judgement or reached a different decision under very slightly different circumstances. Formulas do not suffer from such problems. Given the same input, they always return the same answer' (Kahneman, 2012: 225). In fact, he concludes that: 'The research suggests a surprising conclusion: to maximize predictive accuracy, final decisions should be left to formulas, especially in low-validity environments' (Kahneman, 2012: 225). Based on this, one may now wonder if Expert Forecast = Intuition should be replaced by

Expert Forecast = Model Forecast,

implying that experts should not adjust model forecasts at all. The decision-making literature suggests not, and in fact the suggestion is that 'intuition adds value . . . but only after a disciplined collection of objective information and disciplined scoring of separate traits' (Kahneman, 2012: 231–2). Hence, from the decision-making literature one seems to conclude with Kahneman (2012) that α is perhaps best set at 1, and thus that

Expert-adjusted Forecast = Model Forecast + Adjustment.

Interestingly, as becomes very clear in Chapter 2, this conclusion closely matches the outcome of an econometric perspective on experts adjusting model forecasts, where the optimal adjustment has a few particular properties.

Naturally, the question now is how experts arrive at a numerical value of the adjustment. It can be expected that similar biases to those mentioned above can be at stake when assigning a value to the adjustment. This is true, but perhaps the potential problematic effects of biases can be alleviated by making explicit what is, in an econometric sense, the sign and size of the adjustment. Chapter 2 will start with this issue by proposing that the adjustment should be equal to the expert's knowledge about the future forecast error associated with the model. For example, when the model forecast is equal to, say, 4, and the expert believes that the associated realization will be 1 higher than what might be expected due to, for example, a known future change of policy, then the expert knows part of the future forecast error and can modify the model forecast of 4 to a final expert-adjusted forecast equal to 5. Chapter 2 will also discuss how decisions on the value of that amount of 1 can be made explicit, so that hindsight bias can be alleviated in the future.

EARLY RESULTS

There were a few studies in the late 1980s and the beginning of the 1990s where the authors examined empirical cases where they had expert forecasts, model forecasts and realizations. In a range of studies, Mathews and Diamantopolous (1986, 1989) investigated how experts performed relative to models in terms of out-of-sample forecast accuracy. Their data concerned sales of repeat-purchase products from a manufacturing company in the UK healthcare industry and their main findings were that expert-adjusted forecasts can be better in terms of out-of-sample root mean squared prediction error (RMSPE).

Bunn (1992) provided an overview of the body of knowledge on the synthesis of expert judgement and statistical forecasting, especially in the light of the then emerging concept of decision support systems (DSS) (see also Belsley, 1988 and Fischhoff, 1988). Huss (1986), Edmundson *et al.* (1988) and Willemain (1989) considered cases where forecasts from simple models were subjected to substantial managerial adjustment, apparently with a successful forecast track record. Bunn (1992: 253) concluded that: 'It seems that, while well-specified time series models can be most effective in filtering out noise and projecting past patterns in the data, expert intervention will pay off in practice when there is extra information about new untypical circumstances.' Bunn (1992) also provided a range of reasons why model forecasts might need the adjustment, like low data quality, a change in parameters, omitted variables and the like. There was also an allusion to the notion of somehow combining model forecasts and expert forecasts, which is a strategy that will be analysed below in Chapters 4 and 5. Finally, we may also consider the alternative situation where an initial expert forecast is modified using the information from a model forecast. This interesting situation is, however, beyond the scope of this monograph.

At the beginning of the 1990s, there was also an interest in analysing judgement exercised for macroeconomic forecasts. Drawing on early insights in Howrey *et al.* (1974) and Haitovsky and Treyz (1972), the studies of McNees (1990), Turner (1990) and Donihue (1993) address final expert forecasts for consumer expenditures, gross national product (GNP), exports and inventory investment, to mention a few, when large-scale macroeconomic models delivered the model forecasts.

Donihue (1993: 83) observes that 'virtually none of the macroeconomic forecasting activities in this country [USA] are entirely model-based'. These studies all concern the notion that the model-builders exercise substantial judgement before they arrive at their final model forecast, and it is found that, 'The adjusted forecasts tend to be more accurate overall, although important exceptions are found' (McNees, 1990: 287).

Another important early study is Blattberg and Hoch (1990), who examined expert and model forecasts for catalogue sales of fashion merchandise. They documented that expert-adjusted forecasts can be a little better than model forecasts. In addition, Blattberg and Hoch (1990) showed that when model forecasts and expert forecasts are taken together – that is, somehow combined – their weighted forecast is more accurate. This latter study was for a long time the one that set the agenda, as since then (until recently) almost no studies have appeared where researchers have considered and compared expert-adjusted forecasts with model forecasts. Their 50 per cent model and 50 per cent manager quote (part of the title of their page) was echoed in many later studies.

Quite interestingly, the finding that the 50 per cent/50 per cent rule would work, as a balance of expert and model forecasts, has rarely been disputed. This is particularly relevant as it does matter whether experts have consciously modified model-based forecasts or whether they have ignored them. In other words, the value of α in (1.1) is important before the 50 per cent/50 per cent rule can be recommended. If experts had wholly ignored the model forecast, the 50 per cent/50 per cent rule would indeed seem to be a useful way of combining two independent forecasts based on a model and on pure intuition, respectively. In the case where α is not equal to 0, however, the 50 per cent/50 per cent rule would very much over-weigh the expert input by over-emphasizing the model forecast. Indeed, if the expert simply adds a small number to the model forecast, then the newly combined forecast with a 50 per cent/50 per cent balance would count the model forecast twice. In other words, it very much matters that we know what an expert does, before we can make a claim about a seemingly beneficial 50 per cent/50 per cent rule, as will be discussed in Chapter 5.

A REVIVED INTEREST

Recently, large databases with model forecasts, expert(-adjusted) forecasts and realizations have become available in the areas of macro-economic forecasting and business forecasting, and this has spurred a revived interest in analysing expert-adjusted forecasts. Franses, Kranendonk and Lanser (2011) document that the forecasts from the 1945-founded Netherlands Bureau for Economic Policy Analysis (CPB), which are based on an econometric model of 2,000+ equations, are *all* manually adjusted by domain-specific experts. In sales forecasting, where typically large numbers of forecasts need to be created very frequently, there is, as mentioned, a long tradition of an interaction between forecasting tools and experts. And also, in this latter area, large databases have recently become available (see Fildes *et al.* 2009, and Franses and Legerstee, 2009, 2010), where the first impression is that typically over 95 per cent of all statistical model forecasts are manually modified.

At the same time, research on the evaluation of economic forecasts has intensified. For a long time, researchers usually reported just some statistics on forecast accuracy, but rarely did people bother about which method was more statistically significant than another method. Exceptions are some of the contributions of Clive Granger and co-authors (such as Granger and Newbold, 1986: Chapter 8), but it seems fair to say that a revived focus on forecast evaluation was initiated by Diebold and Mariano (1995). Since then, many studies have appeared on the proper evaluation criteria, how accuracy should be evaluated for rolling-window samples versus recursive samples, and on whether the models are nested or not (Clark and McCracken, 2001, West, 1996, to mention only a few). There are also studies where just plain forecasts are compared, without making assumptions on how they were created (Patton and Timmermann, 2007a, 2007b), but then various specific assumptions – for example, on loss functions – have to be made. All in all, most of the literature requires some knowledge of how the forecasts were created, and this also holds for the situation in the present monograph, where expert-adjusted forecasts and model forecasts are analysed, in the case where experts could have modified the model forecasts.

Intriguingly, in the economics literature there does not seem to be so much interest in understanding how economic forecasts are created. There are plenty of tests on equal forecast accuracy, and there are many forecast competitions where forecasters (the IMF, the Federal Open Market Committee, the OECD and so on) are evaluated, but rarely if ever do analysts worry about the origins of the forecasts. I will claim that these origins do matter, although most diagnostics and tests presume that forecasts are unbiased and created under mean squared error loss. Quite conceivably, such properties do not hold when experts have modified econometric model forecasts. Indeed, sales forecasters may feel that out-of-stock conditions are worse than having enough stock, and hence they may have an asymmetric loss function, which they incorporate in their forecasts (see Chapter 5 below for a discussion). And macroeconomic forecasters may include inappropriate signals from the world economy and overreact, thereby rendering their final forecasts biased. Moreover, when it is known how final forecasts are created, it is also possible to obtain better indications on how future forecasts can be improved, and that can concern model forecasts as well as expert-adjusted forecasts.

GENERAL OUTLINE OF THIS BOOK

This monograph has four key chapters, and they address the following issues. Chapter 2 first outlines what could be viewed from an econometric perspective as the optimal behaviour of experts when they receive model forecasts and can quote their own forecasts. This seems a natural starting point because if we do not know what is the best practice then we cannot give proper guidelines for analysts (and perhaps model-builders and experts). Interestingly, such a discussion on optimal behaviour cannot currently be found in the literature, and hence a few of the guiding principles are summarized here for the first time. One key takeaway from this chapter is that adjusting model forecasts can be a good thing to do, but there is no need to *always* adjust model forecasts, at least when the econometric model is properly specified. As I have said, Chapter 2 takes an econometric perspective and thus does not address other motivations for expert behaviour, such as reputational issues, managerial pressure or even malign motivations.

Chapter 3 then proceeds with a summary of what is currently known about what experts seem to do in practice. This chapter draws on various recent studies that are scattered over many journals and disciplines, and hence this chapter brings together most of the recent evidence into a single chapter. At the same time, it also addresses a few of the earlier findings. One of the main results – and this may not come as a surprise any more – is that most model forecasts are apparently adjusted by experts, whether these forecasts originate from multi-equation macroeconometric models or from simple extrapolation methods. However, this is also surprising, as the so-called 'M competitions' in forecasting (Makridakis and Hibon, 2000) usually document that simple extrapolation rules are among the very best in terms of forecast accuracy, although Hyndman (2013) recently reported obtaining alternative findings. Apparently, the end-users of the forecasts based on simple algorithms tend not to trust these outcomes, as most extrapolation-based forecasts are apparently also modified by experts. The surprise in Chapter 3 is mainly that the frequency of adjusting model forecasts is much higher than one would predict given the theoretical arguments in Chapter 2.

Chapter 4 then reviews the available evidence as to whether expert-adjusted forecasts are any better than model forecasts. This chapter partly draws on a few recent studies involving forecasts for the airline industry, various pharmaceutical firms and for the national economy of the Netherlands. As expert forecasts can encompass model forecasts, one might assume that expert forecasts in some sense nest the model forecasts (which is easily understandable if α in (1.1) is not equal to 0), and hence the evaluation of the expert-adjusted forecasts requires an adaptation of some of the latest advances in methods of evaluating forecast accuracy. In sum, Chapter 4 reports that there is some evidence that expert-adjusted forecasts can be better than model forecasts, but the evidence is limited. At the same time, it is found that when expert-adjusted forecasts are worse, the loss of forecast accuracy is substantial.

Prior to the concluding chapter, Chapter 5 focuses on potential strategies to improve expert-adjusted forecasts and model forecasts. A range of possible strategies (including forecast combinations) are reviewed, and some of these have shown merits in recent empirical settings.

OUTLINE OF THE CHAPTERS AND THE MAIN CONCLUSIONS

As a courtesy to the reader, a few more details of each of the chapters are now provided and a summary of the main findings of this book is presented. Of course, much more research will have to be done in the (near) future, as more and more data become available, but for the moment it seems that the conclusions highlighted below are currently valid.

Chapter 2 deals with the question of whether the adjustment of model forecasts by experts could be a good thing to do, and also in which dimensions this is best done, all taken from an econometric perspective. There are at least three arguments why the adjustment of model-based forecasts can be useful. First, experts may have knowledge about the future forecast errors to be expected due to known structural changes. In a sense, the experts foresee that the next observation – that is, the forecast observation – will contain an outlier component that is somehow known at the time of forecast creation. An example could be the introduction of a new law that becomes effective at the time of the next observation, and which would not have been included in the forecasting model. Second, experts may know more about a possible measurement error in one or more of the explanatory variables. Re-estimation of the model parameters usually does not lead to dramatic changes in the longer-term relation between variables, but it may well be that one of the explanatory variables will experience a large shift. In a sense, this is similar to the notion of a potential forecast error, but here it concerns the forecast value of an explanatory variable. A third reason why expert the adjustment can be beneficial is that in general it can reduce the forecast error, provided that the adjustment is independent of the model forecast. This subtle argument assumes that useful expert adjustment does not replicate what is already in the model, but that the adjustment and the model forecasts are orthogonal to each other. This leads to the first, econometrics-based, conclusion in this monograph:

Conclusion 1:   Theoretically, expert adjustment of model-based fore-
                casts can be relevant and can improve forecast
                accuracy.

Chapter 3 matches the results in Chapter 2 with experts' actually observed behaviour. Theoretically and ideally, the term added to the model forecasts should be independent of the model forecasts and should also be unpredictable. At the same time, α in (1.1) should best be close to or equal to 1. Also, there should be no general theoretical reason for adjusting upwards more often than downwards. A summary of recent empirical results, however, reveals that the current practical behaviour of experts is apparently far from that ideal situation. The differences between expert-adjusted forecasts and model forecasts are often found to be predictable, and experts also favour adjusting upwards much more often than downwards. It is also found that many adjustments are not independent of the model forecasts, meaning that some form of double counting is at stake. Additional to observing their behaviour, we can also simply ask the experts what they do, and then we learn (Boulaskil and Franses, 2009) that experts (from one of the companies studied) themselves say that they quite often ignore the model forecasts and create their own model (with a substantial potential overlap). Also, when observed expert behaviour in terms of the size and sign of the adjustment is associated with personal traits like experience, age and gender, it seems that older experts show signs of over-confidence. So:

Conclusion 2:   The current practice of experts when adjusting model-based forecasts differs from the econometrics-based optimal setting.

Chapter 4 reviews the currently available evidence on whether expert-adjusted forecasts are any better than model-based forecasts in terms of accuracy. Several studies compare accuracy statistics as if the two sets of forecasts are independently compiled, but a few recent studies suggest that the expert-adjusted forecasts might nest (or in a sense extend) the model-based forecasts. Either way, it is generally found that expert forecasts most certainly can improve on model forecasts, but also that such expert-adjusted forecasts can be dramatically poor, which seems to reiterate some of the earlier case-based evidence. Also, there is some evidence that small and infrequent adjustments can be beneficial, although contrasting evidence exists too. At the same time, alternative combinations of expert-adjusted forecasts and model-based forecasts do seem to improve on each of the components. Hence, there seems room for improvement, leading to the third conclusion, which is:

Conclusion 3:   Many expert-adjusted forecasts are not as accurate as they could be.

Given the conclusions of the three previous chapters, Chapter 5 examines various strategies that could improve forecasts (that is, expert-adjusted forecasts, model forecasts and combinations of the two) and bring expert-adjusted forecasts closer to the ideal optimal situation reviewed in Chapter 2. Feedback to the experts on what they apparently seem to do turns out to be helpful, as does the provision of more details of the model. Indeed, most econometric models would allow for a symmetric distribution of the forecast errors, and hence there does not seem to be a need to persistently adjust upwards as experts often seem to do. Also, loss functions of the experts may differ from those of the econometric models, and it can help to formally disconnect the loss function assumed in the forecasting process and the loss function of an expert or manager. Finally, to explicitly include the past judgement of experts in the forecasting models may seem to be helpful too. All this leads to the final conclusion, which is:

Conclusion 4:   There are simple strategies to make final forecasts (much) better.

Finally, Chapter 6 summarizes the main results in (and limitations of) this book, and sketches a range of further research topics. Also, the implications of the findings of this book for experts, model-builders and analysts are discussed.

2   Optimal behaviour of experts

Before analysing the quality of expert-adjusted forecasts, it seems sensible to examine why experts would or should want to adjust model-based forecasts in the first place, this time from an econometric perspective. At the same time, it is relevant to have some kind of benchmark that could be associated with 'optimal' behaviour in an econometric sense. This chapter proposes the notion of such optimal behaviour, where this notion is approached from two different but related angles. The first angle originates from the possibility that a forecast from an econometric model or statistical algorithm may lead to a forecast error of which some part can be expected by an expert: for example, due to a somehow foreseeable regime shift or a sudden change in one of the explanatory variables. The second angle is associated with the prediction errors from the expert-adjusted forecast, which can be shown to be minimized (using a squared loss function) when an expert adds a truly relevant term to the model forecast. This chapter initially deals with one-step-ahead forecasts, but towards the end multiple-steps-ahead forecasts will also be considered.

FUTURE FORECAST ERRORS

To keep the notation simple, it is assumed for the moment that the model that is used to generate one-step-ahead forecasts is the basic Gaussian linear regression model given by

$$y_t = X_t \beta + \varepsilon_t, \quad \text{with} \quad \varepsilon_t \sim N(0, \sigma^2) \tag{2.1}$$

where y_t is the variable to be predicted, with t running from 1 to T, so that T is the forecast origin, where X_t is a $(1 \times K)$ vector with observations on the explanatory variables, with the first element associated with the intercept, β is a $(K \times 1)$ vector with parameters, and where ε_t is a normally distributed error term with constant variance σ^2 and no correlation between leads and lags of ε_t. With available data on the variables y_t and X_t, the parameters can be estimated using ordinary least squares (OLS). It may well be that one or more of the explanatory variables contain the lags of y_t, which then makes the model a so-called econometric time series model. In what follows, it will become clear that the specific type of model that is used to create the model-based forecasts does not matter much for evaluating the expert-adjusted forecasts. Also, the value of K is not important, nor does the number of lagged y_t variables matter. This is all based on the assumption that the expert receives the model forecast and revises this quote, and that he or she is not interfering with one or more of the model components.

Therefore, the subsequent discussion will be continued using a prototypical forecasting model like

$$y_t = \beta_0 + \beta_1 x_t + \alpha y_{t-1} + \varepsilon_t, \quad \text{with} \quad \varepsilon_t \sim N(0, \sigma^2), \tag{2.2}$$

for notational convenience.

When the sample that is used to estimate the parameters runs from 1 to T, then at time T one may wish to create a forecast for one-step-ahead horizon $T + 1$, given the availability of information up to and including T. Denote this forecast as

$$\hat{y}_{T+1|T}. \tag{2.3}$$

Given (2.2), the true observation at time $T + 1$ would be

$$y_{T+1} = \beta_0 + \beta_1 x_{T+1} + \alpha y_T + \varepsilon_{T+1}. \tag{2.4}$$

And, because the true error at time $T + 1$ is unknown at T, the associated one-step-ahead forecast is then

$$\hat{y}_{T+1|T} = \beta_0 + \beta_1 \hat{x}_{T+1|T} + \alpha y_T, \tag{2.5}$$

where for the moment (and for convenience) it is assumed that the parameters are given. In practice these parameters have to be estimated, and this creates additional issues, but these will not be discussed in this monograph. Hence, assuming the values of the parameters and for the moment also assuming that $\hat{x}_{T+1|T}$ is known and equal to x_{T+1} (more on this assumption will appear below), the one-step-ahead forecast error is

$$y_{T+1} - \hat{y}_{T+1|T} = \hat{\varepsilon}_{T+1}. \tag{2.6}$$

Note that in this book the convention is to calculate the forecast error as the realization minus the forecast.

Suppose now that there is an expert with domain knowledge who receives the model-based forecast (2.3), usually without necessarily knowing what the right-hand side of (2.5) looks like. Suppose further that this expert is allowed to manually adjust this model-based forecast. To understand what an expert could optimally do, we need a few more assumptions. The first assumption for the ideal situation is that the model in (2.2) is properly specified. This means that the model contains the appropriate explanatory variables, that the parameters are estimated consistently, and that the errors are uncorrelated over time. Normality is not specifically required, as long as the distribution is symmetric and as long as there are not too many outliers. The second assumption, again for the ideal econometric situation, is that the expert is also convinced that model (2.2) is properly specified. That is, the expert trusts that the model-builder (who is most likely someone other than the expert) knows how the model works, how the variables were selected, and how the parameters were estimated. Now, in practice these assumptions may be very strong, and perhaps implausible, as will be discussed in Chapter 6, but for the moment they benefit the discussion on the ideal econometric situation.

Given these assumptions, it is conceivable that optimal expert adjustment of a model-based forecast as based on (2.5) entails that the expert believes he or she knows part of the forecast error in (2.6), (Franses, 2011a). In other words, the expert believes that he or she can somehow 'model' the future forecast error, such that

$$\hat{\varepsilon}_{T+1} = W_{T+1}\theta_{T+1} + v_{T+1}, \tag{2.7}$$

where W_{T+1} can concern various variables known to the expert and where θ_{T+1} is a time-varying parameter vector, also known to the expert. In individual cases, the error term v_{T+1}, which is not correlated with its leads and lags, does not have to obey a symmetric distribution. The variance of this error term is denoted as σ_v^2, which is smaller than σ^2. Note that the parameters in θ_{T+1} cannot be constant over time, as then the model in (2.2) would not have been properly specified, thus violating the first assumption. Further, (2.7) follows the suggestions from the decision-making literature that the intuition of an expert should be based on rules that can be analysed and evaluated.

Part of $W_{T+1}\theta_{T+1}$ may also be based on the intuition of the expert, but this makes subsequent analysis more difficult as intuition by definition cannot be modelled. Given that $\hat{\varepsilon}_{T+1}$ is not linearly predictable from its own past, as zero correlations with leads and lags were assumed, and also given that v_{T+1} has the same properties, the adjustment term $W_{T+1}\theta_{T+1}$ as in (2.7) is not predictable from its own past, nor can future adjustments be predicted. Based on the assumption that the regression model in (2.2) contains the proper variables, the adjustment $W_{T+1}\theta_{T+1}$ should also not be predictable using the variables in the original econometric forecasting model (2.2) or using any other variables.

Ideally, and on average across many situations, $W_{T+1}\theta_{T+1}$ has mean zero, as that is associated with experts who agree with the notion that the forecast errors in (2.6) are symmetric. Indeed, otherwise an expert may believe that the model is systematically over-predicting or under-predicting.

In sum, given the unbiased model-based forecast, the ideal expert-adjusted forecast thus reads as

$$\hat{y}_{T+1|T}^E = \beta_0 + \beta_1 \hat{x}_{T+1|T} + \alpha y_T + W_{T+1}\theta_{T+1}. \tag{2.8}$$

The expression in (2.8) clearly shows that the expert-adjusted forecast nests the model-based forecast. This will have consequences for evaluating the quality of the expert-adjusted forecasts as one now has to use the methods of Clark and McCracken (2001) (see Chapter 3 below).

Note again that in real-life settings, which can of course contrast with the above ideal setting, there is no need for $W_{T+1}\theta_{T+1}$ to be symmetrically distributed. Hence, it may well be that an expert more often adjusts upwards than downwards. Whether this is beneficial to the quality of the forecasts will be discussed later on. And whether this is perhaps associated with loss functions other than the one underlying least squares estimation will be discussed in Chapter 5. In principle, and on average across many experts, unbiased model forecasts should translate into equally balanced expert adjustments. Also, there is no reason to believe that expert adjustments should be large or particularly small in terms of absolute size, as this relates to the size of the expected forecast error.

A VIEW BASED ON OUTLIERS AT THE FORECAST ORIGIN

An alternative but related view on experts adjusting model-based forecasts is given by the following notion. Consider an expert who has domain knowledge concerning an economic variable Y and who needs to make one-step-ahead forecasts for its realizations y. This expert is aware of the fact that y cannot fully be predicted by its past values, but suppose that, for convenience, as a benchmark model he or she relies on an autoregression of order 1, that is

$$y_t = \beta_0 + \alpha y_{t-1} + \varepsilon_t. \tag{2.9}$$

When considered necessary, the expert can use personal judgement to modify the time series model forecast to give a final adjusted forecast. Such an adjustment can be relevant when the expert knows, as in (2.7), that in the next period there will be a structural level shift that is currently not included in the model. Another reason may be that the expert feels that the most recent observation, which in fact is the observation at the forecast origin for the one-step-ahead forecast, is somehow exceptional. This can be due to a possible shift in the level of the data that has already recently started, or to a single-observation outlier at time T. At the time of producing the forecast the expert has no tools to decide the reason for this exceptional data point, but there may seem to be a need to judgementally adjust the model forecast.

Suppose the expert has data for the variable Y for T consecutive periods (weeks, months, quarters), and denote these as $y_1, y_2, \ldots, y_T$. Observation y_T is the forecast origin, and suppose now that the expert wants to forecast y_{T+1}. Suppose further that the expert considers y_T as exceptional. It can now easily be shown that when the exceptional observation concerns a so-called innovation outlier (IO) (see Fox, 1972 and Franses, 1998: Chapter 6 for the nomenclature), the expert should *not* adjust the forecast. However, when it is a so-called additive outlier (AO) the adjustment could be a function of the forecast error at time T. An explanation follows below.

An innovation outlier at origin T

For ease of notation consider again (2.9) and hence that the observation at time $T + 1$ reads as

$$y_{T+1} = \beta_0 + \alpha y_T + \varepsilon_{T+1}. \tag{2.10}$$

The forecast made at origin T is equal to

$$\hat{y}_{T+1|T} = \beta_0 + \alpha y_T. \tag{2.11}$$

As before, it is assumed that the parameters can be consistently estimated using OLS. Ledolter (1989) has shown that if an exceptional observation (whether it is an IO or an AO, that does not matter) occurs at the forecast origin this does not have much effect on the OLS-estimated parameters. To save notation, hats are only used for forecasts and not for estimated parameters, nor is there a focus on estimation error.

One example of an exceptional observation is an innovation outlier, which when it occurs at the time T can be represented by

$$y_T = \beta_0 + \alpha y_{T-1} + \varepsilon_T + \omega_T, \tag{2.12}$$

where ω_T is defined as equal to ω at time T and equal to 0 at any other time. Assuming that $\omega > 0$, this means that y_T is exceptionally larger at time T even when taking the distribution of ε_T into account. The interesting feature of an innovation outlier is that for the next observation one simply has that

$$y_{T+1} = \beta_0 + \alpha y_T + \varepsilon_{T+1}, \qquad (2.13)$$

and so, when looking back from $T + 1$ to T, there is *nothing exceptional* about y_T when it comes to forecasting the next observation y_{T+1}, while y_T is exceptional when seen from the earlier origin $T - 1$. Hence, in case of an innovation outlier, the expert should *not* adjust the forecast, even though the value of y_T is being thought of as exceptional. At time T it is unknown whether the observation is an IO or not, as there is only a single observation to use for judgement.

An additive outlier at origin T

The discussion changes for the case of a so-called additive outlier at forecast origin T. For the autoregression of order 1 (AR(1)) in (2.9) this would mean that the true observation at T is

$$y_T = \beta_0 + \alpha y_{T-1} + \varepsilon_T \qquad (2.14)$$

but one does not observe realizations of Y but of another (of course related) variable Z, with realization at T equal to

$$z_T = y_T + \omega_T \qquad (2.15)$$

with ω_T again defined as equal to ω at time T and equal to 0 elsewhere. Note that this means that the observed data would correspond with $\{y_{T+1}, z_T, y_{T-1}, y_{T-2}, \ldots\}$. Substituting the AR(1) expression (2.14) gives for the observation at forecast origin T:

$$z_T = \beta_0 + \alpha y_{T-1} + \varepsilon_T + \omega_T, \qquad (2.16)$$

which means that the forecast error at time T, based on a model with parameters estimated for the sample up to and including $T - 1$ data is $\varepsilon_T + \omega$. For horizon $T + 1$ it then holds that

$$
\begin{aligned}
z_{T+1} &= \beta_0 + \alpha z_T + \varepsilon_{T+1} = \beta_0 + \alpha(y_T + \omega) + \varepsilon_{T+1} \\
&= \beta_0 + \alpha y_T + \varepsilon_{T+1} + \alpha\omega.
\end{aligned}
\qquad (2.17)
$$

Thus, for z_{T+1} to become equal to y_{T+1}, which is the true observation without this outlier, the expert would provide the most sensible adjustment if he or she *subtracted* $\alpha\omega$ from the model-based forecast made at time T.

In this case of an additive outlier, and because the expected value of ε_{T+1} is zero, the optimal expert-adjusted forecast thus reads

$$\hat{y}^E_{T+1|T} = \hat{z}_{T+1} - \alpha\omega. \tag{2.18}$$

The question is what is the value of ω? One choice could be to set it equal to the forecast error $\varepsilon_{T|T-1}$, that is, the error observed at time T, when the forecast is made at time $T - 1$. In that case,

$$
\begin{aligned}
\hat{y}^E_{T+1|T} &= \hat{z}_{T+1} - \alpha(\varepsilon_T + \omega)\\
&= \beta_0 + \alpha y_T - \alpha(y_T - \alpha y_{T-1} - \beta_0)\\
&= (1 + \alpha)\beta_0 + \alpha^2 y_{T-1}\\
&= \hat{y}_{T+1|T-1}.
\end{aligned}
\tag{2.19}
$$

So, assuming that the observation itself at time T can be viewed as an additive outlier, and fully adapting for that error, effectively means that the expert-adjusted forecast is the direct two-step-ahead forecast from origin $T - 1$, (see Chevillon, 2007).

Perhaps a more plausible option to calibrate ω (when $\omega > 0$) amounts to considering

$$\hat{\omega} = \hat{\varepsilon}_{T|T-1} - k\sigma \tag{2.20}$$

where σ is the estimated standard error of ε_t and k can be set by the expert.

In sum, *only* when the exceptional observation at time T is an additive outlier, could the adjustment made by the expert result in an improvement in forecast quality. In contrast, when the expert modifies the forecast in case there is not an additive outlier but an innovation outlier, the forecast quality will deteriorate. This result makes judgemental adjustment an intriguing exercise, as at time T one cannot possibly know whether the observation at the forecast origin is an IO or an AO. This in turn suggests that an expert should be hesitant to quickly modify a model-based forecast.

An illustration

To illustrate the above discussion, consider annual growth rates of quarterly real GDP in the Netherlands, for the period 1988Q4 to 2007Q3, retrieved in December 2007 from Statistics Netherlands. The data (in millions of euros) are presented in the Data Appendix Table A1, and graphs of the data together with the growth rates are presented in Figures 2.1 and 2.2, respectively. Growth rates are computed as the natural log of real GDP minus the same observation four quarters ago. The realization in 2007Q3 is 4.1 per cent, and many people in those days viewed this as exceptionally high. Statistics Netherlands also appreciated this by stating that part of the sudden increase in growth rates was perhaps due to unexpectedly increased revenues from natural gas production. The average value of growth per quarter in the total period considered is 2.7 per cent.

A suitable model to describe these data turns out to be an AR(1) model as in (2.9) with parameter a estimated to be equal to 0.834 for the sample ending in 2007Q3 and 0.835 for the sample ending in 2007Q2, thereby supporting the above-mentioned results in Ledolter (1989).

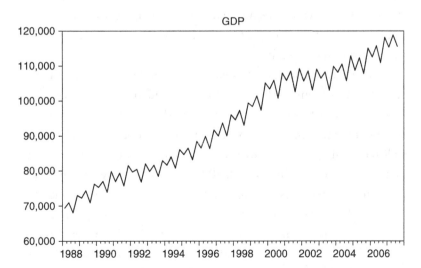

FIGURE 2.1. Real GDP in the Netherlands, 1988Q1–2007Q3, retrieved December 2007 from Statistics Netherlands (in millions of euros).

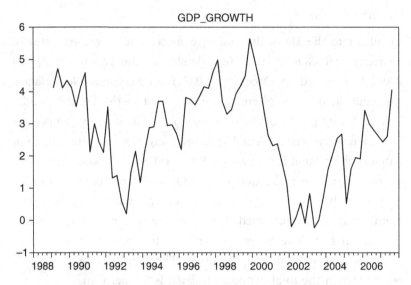

FIGURE 2.2. Annual growth in real GDP in the Netherlands, 1988Q1–2007Q3, retrieved December 2007 from Statistics Netherlands (in percentage points).

The σ is estimated as 0.78 per cent, and the forecast error $\varepsilon_{T|T-1}$ for 2007Q3 is 1.4, which means that the actual realization minus the forecast is 1.4 per cent, which, relative to the estimated standard error, is indeed not small.

The forecast for 2007Q4 based on this AR(1) model would be equal to 3.8 per cent. In that case, the expert adopts the notion that the observation in 2007Q3 is an innovation outlier and does not intervene. Suppose now that the observation at the forecast origin is treated as an additive outlier, which could seem sensible given the added explanation by Statistics Netherlands. If 2007Q3 is fully treated as such, then the adjusted forecast is 3.8–0.834(1.4) = 2.6 per cent. If (2.20) was used, with $k = 1$, the estimated value for ω would be substantial and the adjusted forecast would be 3.8–0.834*(1.4–0.78) = 3.3 per cent. In reality, of course, the expert who adjusts a model-based forecast should have strong arguments for why he or she would want to allow for just one standard deviation.

With hindsight it is perhaps interesting to remark that the revised data (as they were available in January 2014) show that 2007Q4 has a larger growth rate than 2007Q3 (4.8 versus 4.5), and hence, in this particular case, the expert-adjusted forecast based on an AO would have been less accurate than the model-based forecast, and the choice for an IO would have been most accurate.

FUTURE OUTLIERS

The above discussion may seem rather trivial and obvious. However, there are various consequences for carrying out and evaluating judgemental adjustments for model-based forecasts. A key issue here concerns the very nature of an apparently exceptional observation at the forecast horizon and it is then also important how often unexpected data points like these can occur.

Now that it is understood how to properly deal, from an econometric perspective, with an exceptional observation at the forecast origin, the next question is whether such adjustment would help to improve accuracy. This can only be known at time $T + 1$, and hence no sensible statement can be made at the time of making the forecast adjustment. The key reason for this is that one needs to know what kind of exceptional observation y_T was, and this can only be learned afterwards.

The only thing that one *can* do is to study past realizations and to examine whether exceptional data, if there are any, are typically innovation outliers or additive outliers. That is, which types of outliers seem to have occurred regularly? This could give a first impression of what could possibly be happening at time T. Various methods are available for this purpose, and useful examples are the methods outlined in Chen and Liu (1993) and Tsay (1988). Indeed, if only once in a while an *innovation outlier occurs at a forecast origin*, one should not have a strong inclination to adjust the model-based forecast. In fact, adjustment would then lead to poor expert-adjusted forecasts. In contrast, if only once in a while an *additive outlier occurs at a forecast origin*, judgemental adjustment by subtracting or adding a fraction of the recent model-based forecast error should lead to a substantial improvement in forecast quality.

One possible scenario, already discussed at the beginning of this chapter, is that the expert foresees for $T + 1$ the occurrence of an innovation outlier, simply because these have been observed before and some common tendency may be noticeable. Typically this would be associated with an upcoming change in regulations like taxes, or institutional changes like interest rate changes, or with a combination of unusual factors which sometimes happen, like strong stock market dips or rapid oil price increases. In a sense, the expert may then try to forecast the size of the upcoming innovation outlier. Assuming for the moment that only positive exceptional innovations occur, a simple adjustment scheme for the expert to follow now would be to consider the model

$$y_{T+1} = \beta_0 + \alpha y_T + \varepsilon_{T+1} + \omega_{T+1} \tag{2.21}$$

with

$$\omega_{T+1} = \begin{cases} \kappa + \phi W_T + \eta_{T+1}, & \text{if } \omega_{T+1} > 0 \\ 0, & \text{otherwise} \end{cases} \tag{2.22}$$

where W_T covers explanatory variables. Expression (2.22) can be used to deliver

$$\hat{y}^E_{T+1|T} = \beta_0 + \alpha y_T + \hat{\omega}_{T+1}. \tag{2.23}$$

The expression in (2.23) is a so-called censored regression model for the outlier component, and this model (2.21) combined with (2.22) was introduced in Franses and Paap (2002) and is called a censored latent effects autoregression. The expert needs to estimate the values of κ and ϕ and the variance of η, where the choice for the variables in W is also important. When positive and negative innovation outliers occur, one can replace the expression in (2.22) by an expression with two-sided censoring. A useful by-product of this way of formulating what an expert can do is that it helps to keep track of what experts actually do when they modify model forecasts. A plea for keeping track of their behaviour has been made in a variety of studies on judgemental adjustment to forecasts (see Sanders and Ritzman (2001) and Lawrence *et al.* (2006), to mention just a few). In sum, if innovation outliers occur quite frequently, and they are to some extent predictable, one can formulate judgemental adjustment in a censored latent regression framework. This allows for making explicit the judgemental contribution of the expert, and also meets the demands of the decision-making literature (see Kahneman, 2012).

Alternatively, in case of the frequent appearance of additive outliers, one basically has the situation where parts of the observations obey another data-generating process (DGP). To illustrate, consider the following simple DGP for a quarterly observed variable

$$y_t = \alpha + \alpha_1 D_{1,t} + \varepsilon_t, \tag{2.24}$$

where $D_{1,t}$ is a dummy variable which takes the value 1 in quarter 1 and 0 elsewhere for, say, a few years. A graph of such data could look like that displayed in Figure 2.3. So, the mean of the variable is α in quarters 2, 3 and 4, but it is $\alpha + \alpha_1$ in quarter 1 for a few years. The graph

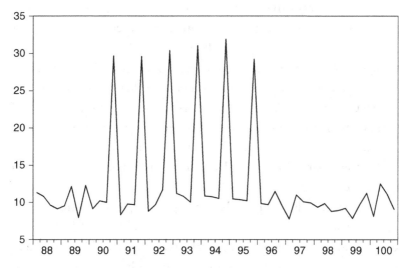

FIGURE 2.3. Infrequent additive outliers, with what seems to be a seasonal pattern.

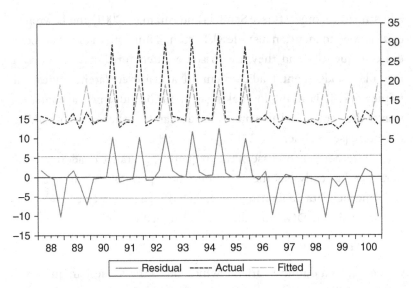

FIGURE 2.4. The fit of a regression of y on four seasonal dummies, and the associated estimated residuals.

of this series would suggest seasonality for a few years, but it can also be viewed as a repetitive sequence of additive outliers.

What would happen if one were to use a constant parameter regression to describe this y_t with four seasonal dummies is visualized in Figure 2.4. The fit of this misspecified model is wholly off-balance, and the estimated residuals display a pattern that is far from normal (see Figure 2.5). Looking at these errors and knowing that the model misses out on an irregular seasonal pattern, the expert thus observes that the model is misspecified as there are so many additive outliers. Hence, the expert will almost always adjust and, in fact, according to a systematic pattern.

Hence, if it is observed that an expert frequently exercises one-sided adjustment (for example, most often upwards), which as we know is not associated with an ideal situation, then this could be in accordance with asymmetries in past model-based forecast errors. And, if it is observed that an expert adjusts almost all the available

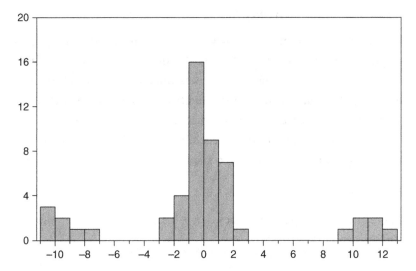

FIGURE 2.5. A histogram of the residuals in Figure 2.4.

model-based forecasts, then, given the time series model used, the data should show many additive outliers, at least in theory. So frequent modification of model-based forecasts is a sign that the expert feels that the model is misspecified, thus violating the second assumption underlying the ideal situation.

Note that these two statements assume that the expert is not just randomly adjusting without any specific reason in mind. Further, it is assumed that the expert sometimes does *not* adjust a model-based forecast. In fact, when there are so many additive outliers, the model *must* be misspecified, and this shall be known to the expert. Note that this does not mean that the expert can claim that *because* the model is a simple time series model it *must* be wrong, as it could well be that just occasional innovation outliers are at stake and hence that on average the model is not bad at all. If the time series model is not useful on its own, then it should be detected from the presence of many additive outliers, and only then can the expert claim that he or she often or almost always has to adjust.

When the model is wrong

When there are too many additive outliers, almost everything goes wrong for a time series model (see Ledolter, 1989; Franses, 1998: Chapter 6). That is, parameters are estimated incorrectly, forecast errors are very large and their distribution is likely to be skewed as the model-based forecasts are biased. Again, the key reason for this is that so many additive outliers basically imply that the model is not properly specified. For example, consider the case

$$x_t = y_t + \omega_t \qquad (2.25)$$

where the Y variable again obeys an AR(1), and where the additive outliers can be described by

$$\omega_t = \alpha + \beta z_t + \eta_t. \qquad (2.26)$$

Writing y_t as $x_t - \omega_t$, one then has

$$x_t - \alpha - \beta z_t - \eta_t = \mu + \rho(x_{t-1} - \alpha - \beta z_{t-1} - \eta_{t-1}) + \varepsilon_t \qquad (2.27)$$

or, equivalently,

$$x_t = \mu + (1 - \rho)\alpha + \rho x_{t-1} + \beta z_t - \rho\beta z_{t-1} + \varepsilon_t + \eta_t - \rho\eta_{t-1} \qquad (2.28)$$

which is a so-called ARMAX(1, 1, 1) model as it includes lagged explanatory variables and it has a first-order autocorrelated error term (which is usually called a moving average variable, abbreviated to MA). Interestingly, this model with an MA component is quite frequently found for macroeconomic time series variables when there are measurement errors (which is, of course, related to additive outliers) (see Granger and Morris, 1976).

So, when additive outliers occur very frequently, this is usually a sign of serious misspecification of the model. It is still possible for an expert to add value based on specific domain knowledge, but (2.28) also indicates that for this added value to lead to better forecasts the expert needs to specify a rather complicated expression based on lagged variables and (perhaps unobserved) error terms. In fact, one could conjecture that it would seem quite unlikely that the expert has *that* much knowledge of the process that he or she is able to construct a proper expert-adjusted forecast based on (2.28). Hence, when there are too many additive outliers, the quality of the adjustment by the expert most likely decreases as the optimal adjustment scheme is very complicated. It is then better to redesign the econometric model or come up with an alternative statistical algorithm.

To sum up, when occasional innovation outliers are going to occur in the future, the expert may be most successful if he or she is somehow able to forecast their values, based on domain-specific information. In contrast, when additive outliers often occur, it seems best to respecify the model, for example by entering additional explanatory variables. These findings may seem trivial, but in practice the analysis of outliers is usually far from that.

Further implications

Given the above results for additive and innovation outliers, it seems that experts' added value to model-based forecasts would be most beneficial to forecast accuracy if experts only have to intervene once in a while. If adjustment is always felt to be needed, then the model is clearly lacking important variables, or something else is wrong. Providing adjustment too often cannot possibly be beneficial, at least from an econometric perspective, and the simple advice should now be that the model needs to be redesigned. Managerial interventions that could be most successful would respond to an additive outlier at the forecast origin, or to a future innovation outlier that is somehow foreseen by the expert. All in all, in principle, the frequency of expert adjustment should be low. Note that the size and the sign of adjustment do not matter much in individual cases, because they depend on the nature of the exceptional observations that can occur. So, observing more positive adjustments done by a single expert is not necessarily a bad sign, as the model that he or she has to rely on may deliver biased forecasts. However, when many experts do so at the same time and when the models at stake deliver unbiased forecasts, then there might be a problematic issue with the model or with the intentions and motivations of the experts.

As useful forecast adjustment should happen only once in a while, at least in the optimal econometric situation, it is quite unlikely that proper expert adjustment can be predicted from the past. Perhaps it would be better to reverse this argument and say that it is *not* a good sign in case the differences between the model-based forecasts and the final expert-adjusted forecasts are predictable from past explanatory variables. That could mean that the econometric time series model is considered by the expert to be seriously misspecified. It could also mean, however, that the expert makes his or her own linear combination of perhaps even the same explanatory variables, which almost by definition cannot come close to the OLS-based linear combinations of variables. One would also not want the experts' added values to be serially correlated, as that would mean that the experts are treating the additive outlier mechanism as an autoregression in itself: for example, if the expert knows that the model forecasts are obtained from

$$y_t = \mu + \rho_1 y_{t-1} + \varepsilon_t. \tag{2.29}$$

But at the same time, if the expert believes that this model is not well specified because it lacks the explanatory variable x, he or she might instead use

$$y_t = \alpha + \lambda_1 y_{t-1} + \beta x_t + u_t \tag{2.30}$$

to create a forecast. For (2.30) it is, however, quite unlikely that $\lambda_1 = \rho_1$. In that case, the added contribution of the expert is

$$\mu - \alpha + (\lambda_1 - \rho_1)y_{t-1} + \beta x_t. \tag{2.31}$$

This added value could be more often positive than negative, and it will also show correlation with leads and lags over time due to y_{t-1}. The additional question here is whether the expert is able to properly calibrate (2.30). All in all, this suggests that the more predictable the adjustment made by the expert, the less likely it is that the final forecast quality is improved. Indeed, it seems best to modify the model first, before it is given to the expert for a final touch. And the less predictable the adjustment by the expert the better the quality of the final forecast will be.

Predicting an explanatory variable

Another argument for experts to manually adjust model-based forecasts, which is closely related with the discussion on outliers above, concerns the potential forecast error induced by the prediction of values for the explanatory variables. Indeed, as (2.5), that is, $\hat{y}_{T+1|T} = \beta_0 + \beta_1\hat{x}_{T+1|T} + \alpha y_T$, already shows, to forecast values for y, one also needs $\hat{x}_{T+1|T}$. This forecast can be based on a model for x, with its associated forecast error, and also there one can encounter peculiarities at or around the forecast origin. Sudden changes in the recent observations on x can lead to manual modification of $\hat{x}_{T+1|T}$ into $\hat{x}_{T+1|T} + b_{T+1}$, together yielding an added term $\beta_1 b_{T+1}$. One may also decide to add a specific term to $\hat{y}_{T+1|T}$ right away.

A further reason to manually adjust model-based forecasts could be that the model parameters are not regularly updated. In many practical situations, researchers rely on recursive or rolling-window estimation techniques, but sometimes the calibration of a large macroeconometric model may be cumbersome and time-consuming. In that case, the parameter estimates are only updated once in a while, and during such a non-updating period something may be added to the model-based forecasts $\hat{y}_{T+1|T}$ to deal with potential changes in the parameter estimates. Detailed discussions on these motivations in the case of the large macroeconometric model developed at the Netherlands Bureau of Economic Policy Analysis (CPB) are presented in Don (2004), Don and Verbruggen (2006), CPB (1992), CPB (2003) and Kranendonk and Verbruggen (2007). Note again that this does not concern the adjustment of the model-builders and it is assumed that their knowledge is included in the model-based forecasts.

Multiple-steps-ahead forecasts

Most of the literature on expert-adjusted forecasts deals with one-step-ahead forecasts, which is perhaps also due to a lack of available practical cases. Another important reason is that very often only one-step-ahead forecasts are at stake, and yet another reason could be that the analysis of multiple-steps-ahead forecasts is not always trivial. For example, consider again the model in (2.2), and consider the true observation at time $T + 2$, which would be

$$
\begin{aligned}
y_{T+2} &= \beta_0 + \beta_1 x_{T+2} + \alpha y_{T+1} + \varepsilon_{T+2} \\
&= \beta_0 + \beta_1 x_{T+2} + \alpha(\beta_0 + \beta_1 x_{T+1} + \alpha y_T + \varepsilon_{T+1}) + \varepsilon_{T+2}.
\end{aligned}
\tag{2.32}
$$

The two-steps-ahead forecast from origin T is thus

$$
\hat{y}_{T+2|T} = \beta_0 + \alpha\beta_0 + \beta_1 \hat{x}_{T+2|T} + \alpha\beta_1 \hat{x}_{T+1|T} + \alpha^2 y_T.
\tag{2.33}
$$

With similar assumptions as for (2.5) the two-steps-ahead forecast error is then

$$
y_{T+2} - \hat{y}_{T+2|T} = \hat{\varepsilon}_{T+2} + \alpha\hat{\varepsilon}_{T+1}.
\tag{2.34}
$$

To manually adjust this two-steps-ahead model forecast the expert needs to have insights into

$$
\hat{\varepsilon}_{T+1} = W_{T+1}\theta_{T+1} + v_{T+1}
\tag{2.35}
$$

jointly with

$$
\hat{\varepsilon}_{T+2} = W_{T+2}\theta_{T+2} + v_{T+2}.
\tag{2.36}
$$

Now, to have knowledge about a range of future forecast errors might indeed be quite difficult. Given these expressions, and again from an econometric perspective, ideally one might expect experts to divert less from long-range model forecasts, simply because not much added information can be available. In Chapter 3 it will be seen whether this indeed occurs in a range of practical cases.

FORECAST ACCURACY

Related to an econometric perspective on expert-adjusted forecasts, there is another recent theoretical result in Legerstee, Franses and Paap (2011) that is worth mentioning. Consider the following potential relation between a model forecast $\hat{y}_{T+1|T}$ and an expert-adjusted forecast $\hat{y}^E_{T+1|T}$, that is,

$$\hat{y}^E_{T+1|T} = \alpha + \beta\hat{y}_{T+1|T} + A_{T+1|T},\tag{2.37}$$

where $A_{T+1|T}$ denotes the adjustment of the expert concerning the observation at $T + 1$, but generated at time T. Note that this term is associated with $W_{T+1}\theta_{T+1}$ as in (2.5).

The question of interest concerns the optimal values of α and β, and the relation between $A_{T+1|T}$ and $\hat{y}_{T+1|T}$. When $\alpha = 0$ and $\beta = 1$, the expert closely follows the model forecast. On average over time, if the model forecasts increase (or decrease) the expert forecasts increase (or decrease) by the same amount. The expert-adjusted forecasts are on average not higher or lower than the model forecasts. The expert-adjusted forecasts are unbiased, just like the model forecasts. The only differences between the expert-adjusted forecasts and the model forecasts are governed by the adjustment. The adjustment is that part of the expert forecast that makes it different from the model forecast. In some sense one may say that this situation where $\alpha = 0$ and $\beta = 1$ is associated with the situation where the expert fully relies on the model forecast, or, if you wish, 'trusts' the model forecast.

When $\alpha \neq 0$ while $\beta = 1$, the expert forecasts are on average higher (when $\alpha > 0$) or lower (when $\alpha < 0$) than the model forecasts. There is a constant difference between the expert and model forecasts. One potential reason for this outcome could be that the expert has an alternative loss function. For example, for the expert it may hold that over-predicting is worse than under-predicting (see also Chapter 5 below).

When $\alpha = 0$ and $0 < \beta < 1$, a change in the model forecasts dampens the expert forecast. The expert may feel that the model forecasts are moving in the right direction but do so too much, and hence a dampening factor is imposed.

Of course, an extreme variant is the case where $\alpha = 0$ and $\beta = 0$. In that case, the expert forecast is fully based on intuition (see Chapter 1).

Legerstee, Franses and Paap (2011) proceed with a discussion of which factors may cause the values of α and β to differ from 0 and 1, respectively. Additionally, and this adds to the discussion in the current chapter, the authors derive a few theoretical implications of the values of α and β for forecast accuracy. For convenience, they use the expected squared prediction error (ESPE) criterion when comparing expert-adjusted forecasts with model forecasts. Their key results are that the improvement in the expected forecast accuracy of the expert-adjusted forecast over that of the model forecast increases when

(i) $\alpha = 0$, or when α gets close to 0
(ii) $\beta = 1$, or when β gets close to 1
(iii) the correlation between $A_{T+1|T}$ and $\hat{y}_{T+1|T}$ is minimal or absent.

In sum, the optimal expert-adjusted forecast reads as

$$\hat{y}^{E}_{T+1|T} = \hat{y}_{T+1|T} + A_{T+1|T}, \tag{2.38}$$

with $\hat{y}_{T+1|T}$ orthogonal to $A_{T+1|T}$. Note that (2.38) closely matches the notion obtained from the decision-making literature as discussed in Chapter 1.

CONCLUSION

This chapter has shown that there are various good reasons for experts to manually adjust model-based forecasts. These reasons can be data-based, based on foreseeable structural changes, or the result of delayed updates of parameter estimates. When they are properly done, one can also expect that expert-adjusted forecasts will provide higher forecast will accuracy than model-based forecasts.

For expert-adjusted forecasts to provide most accuracy, and also to adhere to an optimal situation from an econometric perspective, the expert-adjusted forecasts should be of the form

Expert-adjusted Forecast = Model Forecast + Adjustment.

Importantly, the adjustment component should be unpredictable from its own past or from other variables, while at the same time it should have mean zero, on average. Also, the adjustment should be independent of the model forecast.

The next chapter surveys the available evidence on the relation between expert-adjusted forecasts and model-based forecasts. Based on a variety of empirical results, it shall be documented that this ideal situation rarely seems to appear in practice, at least at present.

3   Observed behaviour of experts

The previous chapter ended with a description of the (econometric) properties of optimal expert adjustment, given that an expert has received a statistical model forecast, which he or she could incorporate in the expert-adjusted forecast. In the present chapter some of the currently available and recent empirical evidence of expert adjustment is reviewed. This chapter consists of three sections. First, a review of empirical results is given for such diverse companies and institutions as KLM (Royal Dutch Airlines), Bayer and Organon (both pharmaceutical companies) and the CPB (the Netherlands Bureau of Economic Policy Analysis). The results of various other available studies will also be included. Next, there is a brief discussion on what experts themselves say that they apparently do, based on anecdotal evidence and also based on interviews with the experts from Organon. Finally, this chapter deals with possible explanatory variables for the observed behaviour of the experts like personal traits (age and experience) and job characteristics (how often the experts make the forecasts).

The key lesson to be learned from the evidence summarized in this chapter is that there are substantial differences between the optimal behaviour as put forward in Chapter 2 and the observable behaviour of experts. Moreover, there seem to be various explanatory variables to predict this behaviour, and these are predominantly associated with past behaviour, past realizations and past forecasts. Personal traits do not seem to matter much.

EMPIRICAL EVIDENCE OF BEHAVIOUR

This first section deals with some of the recently available empirical evidence in the literature, and it also provides various new and never before published results.

KLM

With the help of two senior staff members of KLM Royal Dutch Airlines (KLM for short), a unique database was acquired. It contains the monthly airline revenue data for the period from April 2004 up to and including December 2008 for KLM for seven distinct regions and for the world as a whole. The regions are Europe, the Middle East, Africa, North America, Latin and South America, Asia Pacific and India. Forecasts for these revenue data are created for three months, two months and one month ahead. For one month (April 2006) the data are missing. Unfortunately, the data cannot be displayed in the Data Appendix for confidentiality reasons. The forecasts are all made by experts who base their final forecasts on input from model forecasts, but to what extent they do so is unknown to the analyst (the author of this book). In fact, the statistical model forecasts are not available and hence an approximation method must be considered.

Figure 3.1 displays total revenues and various forecasts. Clearly there is generally an upward trend, with a noticeable decline at the end of the sample, corresponding with the worldwide economic crisis that started in the second half of 2008. Also, one can see a strong seasonal pattern in the data. Furthermore, all forecasts seem to be quite accurate, with slightly larger forecast errors towards the end of the sample.

A first analysis of the expert-adjusted forecasts is based on a simple regression of the realizations on a constant and the forecasts. Consider the availability of (the natural logs of) actual airline revenue data y_t and consider the expert forecasts for these data made at time $t-1, t-2, \ldots, t-h$ denoted as $\hat{y}^E_{t|t-h}$, where h is 1, 2 and 3. The commonly applied auxiliary test regression to diagnose potential bias in these forecasts is

$$y_t = \alpha + \beta \hat{y}^E_{t|t-h} + u_t. \tag{3.1}$$

The null hypothesis of no bias corresponds with

$$\alpha = 0, \quad \beta = 1 \tag{3.2}$$

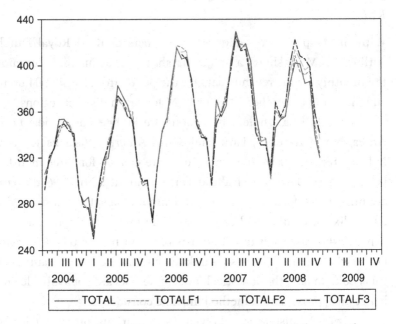

FIGURE 3.1. Total airline revenue and forecasts created three months, two months and one month ago.

in (3.1). The forecasts $\hat{y}^E_{t|t-h}$ are created by experts, who may have used a statistical model and/or publicly available variables. Alternative to (3.2) are the cases where $\alpha > 0$, $\beta < 1$, which implies that the forecasts are too high, on average, and $\alpha < 0$, $\beta > 1$, which implies that the forecasts are too low, on average.

Table 3.1 presents the estimation results for a regression model (3.1) for the total revenues, where the raw data have been transformed by taking natural logarithms to dampen the variance. Comparing the estimates with the standard errors, it is clear that the estimates for α are slightly different from 0, while the estimates for β are slightly different from 1. The Wald test values in the final column of Table 3.1 suggest that there is some modest evidence (at the 10 per cent level) of bias in these expert(-adjusted) forecasts.

The cells in Table 3.2 show that the revenue forecasts for Europe and Latin and South America are all unbiased. In contrast, substantial

Table 3.1: *Testing for bias in expert forecasts, total revenues (estimated standard error in parentheses)*

Horizon	α	β	Wald test (p-value)
Three months	0.338 (0.164)	0.942 (0.028)	4.285 (0.117)
Two months	0.328 (0.150)	0.944 (0.026)	4.766 (0.092)
One month	0.245 (0.117)	0.958 (0.020)	4.804 (0.091)

Test regression is:
$$\log y_t = \alpha + \beta \log \hat{y}^E_{t|t-h} + u_t$$
and the Wald test concerns the null hypothesis that $\alpha = 0, \beta = 1$. The sample size is 54 (not 55 due to missing a missing observation) 56 and 57, for forecast horizons 3, 2 and 1, respectively.

bias for all three horizons is found for the Middle East and India. Forecasts for North America show bias for the horizons 3 and 1, which is unexpected, as one might wish to achieve less bias with shorter horizons, as appears to be the case for most expert forecasts. Finally, two-months-ahead forecasts for Africa also show bias. In sum, out of the $7 \times 3 = 21$ cases, eleven show bias. Note that for all these eleven cases it holds that $\alpha > 0, \beta < 1$. In other words, in the cases with bias the expert(-adjusted) forecasts are too high. And when a range of unbiased econometric model forecasts were available, underlying the expert forecasts, the experts seemed to generally adjust upwards.

The statistics in Table 3.3 show that the bias in the total sales forecasts can be associated with skewed distributions of the forecast errors, that is, the expert(-adjusted) forecasts indeed tend to be too high. The negative skewness becomes smaller when the forecast horizon decreases, which is a result that one would hope to see in practice. The absolute value of the minimum forecast errors is larger than that of the maximum forecast errors, showing that not only can the forecasts be more often too high, but when they are higher they are more so (in an absolute sense) than when they are lower. These results are amplified in Table 3.4, where the same holds for (almost)

Table 3.2: *Testing for bias in expert forecasts, revenue data for seven regions (standard error in parentheses). Numbers in boldface indicate significance at the 5 per cent level*

Region	Horizon	α	β	Wald test (p-value)
Europe	3	0.135 (0.136)	0.970 (0.029)	2.094 (0.351)
	2	0.171 (0.125)	0.963 (0.026)	3.459 (0.177)
	1	0.156 (0.093)	0.967 (0.020)	2.998 (0.223)
Middle East	3	0.939 (0.233)	0.694 (0.075)	17.76 **(0.000)**
	2	0.789 (0.208)	0.743 (0.067)	15.20 **(0.001)**
	1	0.576 (0.173)	0.813 (0.056)	11.37 **(0.003)**
Africa	3	0.213 (0.131)	0.944 (0.035)	4.012 (0.135)
	2	0.307 (0.123)	0.919 (0.033)	10.18 **(0.006)**
	1	0.072 (0.111)	0.982 (0.030)	1.546 (0.462)
North America	3	0.323 (0.118)	0.924 (0.028)	10.12 **(0.006)**
	2	0.256 (0.116)	0.939 (0.028)	5.470 (0.065)
	1	0.283 (0.109)	0.933 (0.026)	8.512 **(0.014)**
Latin and South America	3	0.057 (0.137)	0.986 (0.039)	1.710 (0.425)
	2	0.042 (0.135)	0.991 (0.038)	1.537 (0.464)
	1	−0.050 (0.115)	1.017 (0.033)	2.351 (0.309)
Asia Pacific	3	0.697 (0.191)	0.833 (0.045)	14.13 **(0.001)**
	2	0.559 (0.162)	0.867 (0.038)	12.32 **(0.002)**
	1	0.304 (0.126)	0.928 (0.030)	5.804 (0.055)
India	3	0.300 (0.095)	0.835 (0.049)	13.15 **(0.001)**
	2	0.273 (0.082)	0.848 (0.042)	16.15 **(0.000)**
	1	0.251 (0.080)	0.860 (0.042)	14.23 **(0.000)**

Test regression is: $\log y_t = \alpha + \beta \log \hat{y}^E_{t|t+h} + u_t$ and the Wald test concerns the null hypothesis that $\alpha = 0$, $\beta = 1$. The sample size is 54, 56 and 57, for forecast horizons 3, 2 and 1, respectively.

all seven regions. In eighteen of the twenty-one cases, the skewness is negative. For Europe, Africa and Asia Pacific we see a strong and steady decrease in skewness from horizons 3 to 1, but for other regions this is not the case.

Table 3.3: *Properties of forecast errors* $y_t - \hat{y}^E_{t|t-h}$, *total revenue data*

Horizon	Mean	Minimum	Maximum	Skewness	Kurtosis
Three months	-0.352	-22.00	20.99	-0.493	3.345
Two months	-0.281	-21.70	17.34	-0.180	2.891
One month	0.424	-15.03	14.46	-0.050	3.000

The sample size is 54, 56 and 57, for forecast horizons 3, 2 and 1, respectively.

Table 3.4: *Properties of forecast errors* $y_t - \hat{y}^E_{t|t-h}$, *sales data for seven regions*

Region	Horizon	Mean	Minimum	Maximum	Skewness
Europe	3	-0.518	-10.00	7.800	-0.052
	2	0.587	10.30	6.500	-0.161
	1	-0.171	-5.800	5.850	0.043
Middle East	3	-0.192	-3.200	2.880	0.055
	2	-0.128	-2.400	2.180	0.186
	1	-0.070	-2.600	1.760	-0.250
Africa	3	0.238	-3.840	3.270	-0.573
	2	0.384	-2.800	3.000	-0.264
	1	0.191	-3.440	3.800	-0.018
North America	3	0.475	-5.800	5.020	-0.402
	2	0.214	-6.000	5.610	-0.482
	1	0.360	-8.400	4.990	-1.151
Latin and South America	3	0.345	-3.810	3.890	-0.086
	2	0.341	-4.710	4.330	-0.382
	1	0.356	-3.270	3.020	-0.236
Asia Pacific	3	-0.550	-12.80	6.160	-0.999
	2	-0.347	-10.10	8.690	-0.593
	1	-0.101	-7.400	4.760	-0.584
India	3	-0.151	-1.900	1.400	-0.364
	2	-0.159	-1.911	1.000	-0.862
	1	-0.141	-2.010	0.950	-0.809

The sample size is 54, 56 and 57, for forecast horizons 3, 2 and 1, respectively.

In sum, when the KLM experts included econometric model-based forecasts, their adjustment was most often upwards. Anecdotal evidence obtained when discussing these findings with the two senior staff members of KLM confirms the noticed tendency to adjust upwards. In 2008 when the market went down quickly, it was considered better to inform top management about this downturn when spread out over a few months. Hence, instead of a forecast with, say, a 12 per cent downturn, a range of subsequent forecasts were turned down, each with, say, 4 per cent. In Chapter 4 these KLM expert forecasts will be considered again to see whether they are better than the model forecasts that will be newly created by the analyst, using publicly available information.

Does adjustment occur more often upwards than downwards?

These results for KLM seem to suggest that in practice one could find that expert adjustment is more often upwards than downwards. In their seminal work, as they were the first to address managerial intervention in business forecasting based on actual empirical data and not on experiments with students, Mathews and Diamantopoulos (1986) and Diamantopoulos and Mathews (1989) show that of their 281 cases, 236 forecast revisions were upwards (1986: Table 4) and only 45 were downwards. Recent empirical evidence based on a multitude of cases seems to reiterate this early finding. In their often-cited seminal paper, Fildes *et al.* (2009) consider data at the stock keeping unit (SKU) level for four companies (pharmaceuticals, food, household products and a retailer) for which they have more than 60,000 forecasts and realizations, all at the one-step-ahead level. The results in their Table 3 (2009: 9) show that for the first three companies (pharmaceuticals, food and household products) the fraction of cases with no expert adjustment is 3,174/10,579 = 30 per cent of the cases, and hence in 70 per cent of the cases experts see reasons to deviate from model forecasts. Of these 70 per cent cases, in 54 per cent of those cases the expert adjustment is positive while in 46 per cent it is negative. Given the sheer size of the database, these numbers (54 per cent and 46 per cent) are significantly different from 50 per cent. For their retailer database in most situations there is no adjustment (90 per cent), but when there is adjustment it is positive in 56 per cent of the cases.

De Bruijn and Franses (2012) analyse twenty-nine monthly three-steps-ahead forecasts for 2,472 products created by sixty-seven experts associated with Bayer (the German pharmaceutical company based in Leverkusen). Their Table 4 reports on two different types of forecasters, about which more will be said below, and these two types provide upward adjustments in 63.3 per cent and 61.4 per cent of the cases.

Organon

Franses and Legerstee (2009, 2011a) study the properties of one-step-ahead to twelve-steps-ahead forecasts for SKU sales data for the Netherlands-based pharmaceutical company Organon. At present, this company operates under a different name (Merck, Sharp and Dohme, January 2014), but the data concern the period when the company was still called Organon. Monthly data are available from October 2004 up to and including October 2006 for a range of products within seven general product categories. The number of triplets – that is, expert-adjusted forecasts – model-based forecasts and the actual realizations is more than 30,000. To create their forecasts, Organon relied on an adapted version of ForecastPro™, a professional forecasting tool, where the input to the forecasting algorithms consists of lagged sales data for the particular product. To obtain an impression of the type of data analysed, consider Figure 3.2, which shows that there can be substantial differences between the three elements of the triplets. Additionally, the data show substantial variation, which suggests that they might be associated with what Kahneman (2012: 225) calls a 'low-validity environment'.

Franses and Legerstee (2009) consider only one-step-ahead forecasts and their Table 1 (2009: 38) shows that on average in 89.5 per cent of the cases expert adjustment (in that paper defined as the difference between the expert forecast and the model forecast) is not equal to 0. Table 2 in that same paper documents that, on average, the fraction of

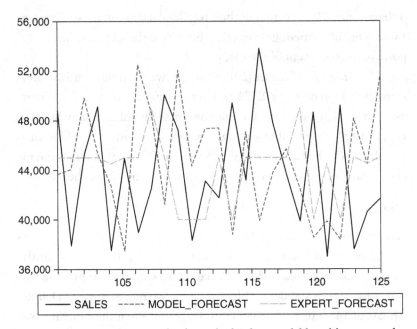

FIGURE 3.2. An example of actual sales data, model-based forecasts and expert-adjusted forecasts. The data concerns sales (in units) of a pharmaceutical product sold from October 2004 upto and including October 2006, which entails twenty-five monthly observations.

upward expert adjustment is 53.5 per cent, which is in strong accordance with the results in Fildes *et al.* (2009). When the analysis is confined to only those cases where all one-step-ahead to twelve-steps-ahead forecasts are available, Franses and Legerstee (2011a: 543, Table A1) show that the fraction of non-zero expert adjustments is as high as 95 per cent. Remarkably, and in contrast to the optimal situation discussed in Chapter 2, this fraction is constant over the forecast horizons. Indeed, given the increased complexity of adding something meaningful to a model-based forecast, one would have predicted that the number of cases with zero adjustment would increase with the horizon. The same authors also compute the average absolute percentage difference (AAPD) between expert adjusted forecasts and model-based forecasts, and their tabular results are presented in Figure 3.3. The fitted line corresponds with the regression of the

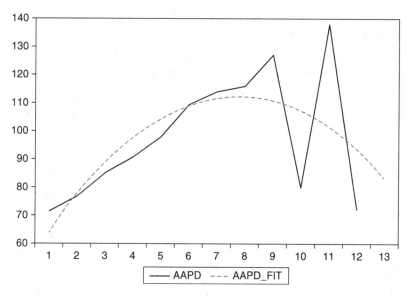

FIGURE 3.3. Average absolute percentage differences (AAPD) between expert forecasts and model forecasts and the fit of a regression of AAPD on an intercept, horizon and horizon squared.

AAPD on the horizon and the horizon squared. Clearly, there seems to be a peak of AAPD around horizons 6 and 7. Interestingly, this turns out to be the most important forecast horizon for Organon's managers (experts), which seems to be due to the average shipping time of the products across the globe.

CPB

The Netherlands Bureau for Economic Policy Analysis (CPB) employs a large macroeconomic model to create forecasts for a range of important macroeconomic variables. The current CPB model contains 2,000+ equations, and 30+ of these equations require estimation methods for the key parameters. In other words, many equations are definitions or equalities. The CPB model is used for various purposes, and one of these is to generate forecasts for key macroeconomic variables like GDP, employment, exports, imports and inflation. The forecasts concern annual observations in year $T + 1$, while the forecast origins are the four quarters in year T. The forecasts are based on real-time observations of the explanatory variables.

As discussed in Franses, Kranendonk and Lanser (2011), the econometric model forecasts from the CPB model never make it to the general public straightaway, which means that non-zero expert adjustment is 100 per cent. This seems to match the discussion in Chapter 1 concerning the early evidence on macroeconomic forecasting. Before they are published in the quarterly publications of the CPB, the model-based forecasts are scrutinized by various experts who assess the accuracy and adequacy of the model forecasts, and who suggest judgemental adjustments. Only these expert-adjusted forecasts are made publicly available and are considered as input by governmental policymakers.

Interestingly, and in contrast with other forecasting areas, the CPB has kept track (at least since 1997) of the nature and size of their adjustments, and they also store information about the econometric models used. At the CPB all experts first receive the forecasts from the model and after that they decide on adjusting these forecasts.

Expert adjustment at the CPB occurs via so-called add factors which are imposed on one or more equations, and which, via other equations, can have an effect on the final forecast. Furthermore, the documentation available at the CPB makes it possible to re-create the original model forecasts, as these were unfortunately not stored throughout the years. The authors (Franses, Krandendonk and Lanser, 2011) mention that they spent half a year obtaining the original forecasts by re-running the original models.

More specifically, for its short-term and medium-term macroeconomic forecasts the CPB relies on a large-scale econometric reduced-form model, containing about 50 estimated behavioral equations, about 150 'rules of thumb' for various equations, and about 2,400 technical and accounting identities. Each quarter, CPB publishes a short-term forecast for the Dutch economy, which results from several iterative model runs. The model-builders play a prominent role in this forecasting process. First, they provide historical input data for the past. Second, they provide forecasts for the necessary exogenous variables for the forecasting period, covering, for example, world trade, oil prices, import prices, tax rates and social security premiums. Third, they propose model adjustments which accommodate a potentially changing economic environment.

Table 1 of Franses, Krandendonk and Lanser (2011: 484) shows the means of the differences between expert-adjusted forecasts and model forecasts for ten key economic variables in the Netherlands and the four quarters in which these forecasts were created. In eight of the forty cases the average value is negative, meaning that in 80 per cent of the cases the expert adjustments are positive, at least on average.

To summarize the insights from this chapter so far, based on the currently available evidence (KLM, Bayer, Organon and CPB) for a range of forecast situations (variables, forecast horizons and sampling frequency), it seems that the dominant sign of expert adjustments is positive. Hence, more model-based forecasts are adjusted upwards than downwards. The available literature presents figures that range from 54 per cent to about 80 per cent. At the same time, the literature also shows that quite often the model-based forecasts are even sometimes adjusted in 100 per cent of the cases, and quite often close to 90 per cent of the cases. As the optimal situation described in Chapter 2 predicts that expert adjustment should not be frequent, and that on average it should equal zero, the empirical evidence so far suggests that this (econometric) optimal situation is not currently encountered in practice.

Are adjustments more often upwards because the model forecasts are biased?

It could be that managers revise model-based forecasts upwards because they have learned that model forecasts tend to be too low. Indeed, looking back at the first study in this area, Table 2 in Mathews and Diamantopoulos (1986) shows that the model forecasts are below the actual realization in no less than 196 of the 281 cases. These authors mention (1986: 5) that a version of Holt's two-parameter exponential smoothing model is used, and apparently this model delivers biased forecasts because 70 per cent of the model forecasts are too low. At the same time, their Table 2 shows that the revised forecasts ('manipulated' in their wording) are too high in 184 of the 281 cases, which is 65 per cent of the cases. Hence, their managers or experts seem to overdo it a little bit in their compensation of potential model bias.

Using the large Organon database, and after some aggregation, Table 2 of Franses and Legerstee (2011b: 2367) shows that the one-step-ahead model forecasts are larger than the realizations in 49.5 per cent of the cases, which suggests that the algorithms used by Organon do not deliver biased forecasts. At the same time, the expert-adjusted forecasts are larger than the model-based forecasts in 55.9 per cent of the cases. Also, for two-steps-ahead to twelve-steps-ahead forecasts, Franses and Legerstee (2011b) document that the model-based forecasts for the Organon sales data are all unbiased. So, in general, no persistent upwards adjustment seems to be necessary in that case.

Using the test method of (3.1), Franses, Kranendonk and Lanser (2011: 486, Table 4) analyse the model forecasts for ten macroeconomic variables, for four forecast origins and for two data releases. In thirty-five of these eighty cases, it is found that there is significant forecast bias at the 5 per cent level. This number reduces to eleven of the eighty cases when the expert-adjusted forecasts are considered (2011: Table 5). So, for the macroeconomic examples, it can happen that experts adjust upwards because model forecasts seem to have a downward bias. Strictly speaking, model forecasts based on variants of the regression model, with symmetrically distributed errors, should not be significantly off-target. Hence, apparently the CPB model includes components that do cause forecast bias.

Hence, yes, it may be that expert-adjusted forecasts are exceeding model-based forecasts due to presumed bias in the model forecasts, but this seems to be confined to isolated cases. The results from Organon's extensive database indicate that such a model bias does not exist, which seems to meet the first important assumption underlying the theoretical discussion in Chapter 2.

Is expert adjustment predictable?

The main conclusion of Chapter 2 was that for expert-adjusted forecasts to provide most accuracy, and also to adhere to an optimal situation (in an econometric sense), the expert-adjusted forecasts should be of the form

Expert-Adjusted Forecast = Model Forecast + Adjustment,

that is, the weight of the model forecast is equal to 1. And the adjustment should not be predictable from its own past or from other variables, while at the same time it should preferably have mean zero, when averaged over many cases.

There are various ways of diagnosing whether this optimal situation holds in practice, at least approximately. Franses, Kranendonk and Lanser (2011) consider the auxiliary regression (in analogy with Blattberg and Hoch, 1990), which reads as:

$$\hat{y}^E_{T+1|T} = \mu + \rho\hat{y}_{T+1|T} + \varepsilon_{T+1}, \tag{3.3}$$

where they examine the joint null hypothesis that $\mu = 0$, $\rho = 1$. Indeed, under this null hypothesis the variable $\hat{y}^E_{T+1|T} - \hat{y}_{T+1|T}$ is uncorrelated with $\hat{y}_{T+1|T}$ under the assumption that $\hat{y}_{T+1|T}$ is uncorrelated with the error term. Note that when the model forecast $\hat{y}_{T+1|T}$ and the error term ε_{T+1} are correlated, which could be the case when experts add adjustment after seeing the model forecasts, and where the added term correlates with the model forecasts, then a key assumption of ordinary least squares (OLS) is violated and one instead has to resort to instrumental variables (IV) estimation. Legerstee, Franses and Paap (2011) adopt this strategy but find qualitatively similar results as the OLS outcomes for the Organon database, namely that $\hat{y}^E_{T+1|T} - \hat{y}_{T+1|T}$ is predictable to some extent, depending on the type of explanatory variables to be included.

Using (3.3), Franses, Kranendonk and Lanser (2011) show that out of forty cases (four forecast origins and ten variables) there are twenty-four cases where the null hypothesis that $\mu = 0$, $\rho = 1$ is rejected at the 5 per cent level. The same study also considers two alternative methods to diagnose predictability, and these are based on the auxiliary regressions

$$\hat{y}^E_{T+1|T} - \hat{y}_{T+1|T} = \mu + \rho(\hat{y}^E_{T|T-1} - \hat{y}_{T|T-1}) + \nu_{T+1}, \tag{3.4}$$

where current adjustment is correlated with one-period-lagged adjustment, and

$$(\hat{y}^E_{T+1|T} - \hat{y}_{T+1|T})^2 = \mu + \rho(\hat{y}^E_{T|T-1} - \hat{y}_{T|T-1})^2 + \nu_{T+1}, \tag{3.5}$$

where current adjustment squared is correlated with one-period lagged squared adjustment. In Franses, Kranendonk and Lanser (2011: Table 2), it is documented that for (3.4) the ρ is estimated as significantly different from 0 at the 5 per cent level in four cases and in no cases for (3.5). So, in the case of the macroeconomic variables considered here, the difference between expert-adjusted forecast and the model forecast, that is, $\hat{y}^E_{T+1|T} - \hat{y}_{T+1|T}$, is to some extent predicted by the model forecast $\hat{y}_{T+1|T}$, but there seems to be no persistence in these adjustments, according to an analysis of (3.4) and (3.5).

The results in Franses and Legerstee (2009) for the SKU-level sales data of the large pharmaceutical company Organon are very different, however. As the observations show large variation in size, these authors choose to model the relative adjustments, that is,

$$100\frac{\hat{y}^E_{T+1|T} - \hat{y}_{T+1|T}}{\hat{y}_{T+1|T}}. \tag{3.6}$$

Given the larger time series sample in this case, Franses and Legerstee (2009) can consider regressing the variable in (3.6) on its own lags 1, 2 and 6, and also on lags 1, 2 and 6 of

$$100\frac{\hat{y}_{T+1|T} - y_{T+1}}{y_{T+1}}, \tag{3.7}$$

which are the model-based forecast errors, expressed as percentages, and they also include a few squared terms. The sum of the parameters for the autoregressive terms is interpreted as persistence, and the total effect of the model-based forecast errors is measured by the sum of the three parameters associated with lags of the expression in (3.7). Their Table 4 shows that the average R^2 of this regression is 0.443 (averaged over 200+ country/product category combinations). Their Table 5 shows that the persistence is on average 0.773, while the total effect of past model-based forecasts errors is 0.226 (Table 6). Hence, there is a strong positive autocorrelation in expert adjustments, which, as Chapter 2 explained, may be interpreted in an econometric sense as that the experts believe that the model is misspecified. Using the same explanatory variables, but now to explain the sign of the expert adjustment, Franses and Legerstee (2009: Table 7) show that the McFadden R^2 is on average 0.289, which is quite high for binary (logit) regression models.

In sum, these results for the SKU sales forecasts show that the size and sign of adjustment $\hat{y}^E_{T+1|T} - \hat{y}_{T+1|T}$ can be predicted from the observable past to a large extent. This seems to be in sharp contrast with the optimal situation, in an econometric sense.

Does the law of small numbers prevail?

In arriving at their forecasts, experts go through a decision-making process that is similar to decision-making by people like gamblers and investors. There is an information set, and the decision-maker has to judge whether there is reason to act. Here an expert sees the model-based forecast, and also has information on variables that might need inclusion in a final forecast, at least in the expert's opinion. The extent of that action again depends on judgement. Like investors and gamblers, the success rate of the decision is quickly noticeable. Forecasts can be matched with realizations, and a horse race between models and experts can be run, as will be done in Chapter 4 for the present examples.

There is much literature on the behaviour of gamblers and financial investors, and one aspect of their behaviour has been recently summarized in Rabin (2002). See also Camerer (1989), De Bondt and Thaler (1987) and Durham, Hertzel and Martin (2005) for detailed empirical results. This aspect is that the behaviour of these actors obeys the law of small numbers (LSN), a regularity first addressed by Tversky and Kahneman (1971), and also addressed in Kahneman (2012: Chapter 10). To quote Rabin (2002), the LSN entails that people 'exaggerate how likely it is that a small sample resembles the parent population from which it is drawn'.

Now it could be that the behaviour of experts who adjust model-based forecasts also obeys the LSN. Experts receive the model-based forecast, and when a large observation occurs, they likely overlook the fact that the effect of this observation is captured by new recursive estimates of the model parameters by newly updated model-based forecasts. So they might keep on adjusting model-based forecasts for too long. Additionally, specific information included in the adjustment could be interpreted as being relevant for future forecasts more often and longer than necessary. Indeed, shocks are typically absorbed in new values of the variable to be predicted. In sum, experts who adjust model-based forecasts could be prone to seeing changes in levels and trends based on recent events, which are not there for long and are already incorporated into the updated recursive model forecasts.

Even though there is a large literature on the LSN for gamblers and investors, there is not an overwhelming amount of empirical documentation. Perhaps this is due to the fact that LSN-like behaviour is difficult to observe from actual behaviour. In the case of experts who adjust model-based forecasts, a simple methodology can, however, be designed to elicit this behaviour, provided one has the proper data.

The line of thought is as follows. When an expert incorrectly believes there is a changing trend or level, he or she will consequently incorrectly predict future events at some fixed event horizon h, and it does not matter if that horizon comes closer or not. So, if one combines fixed-event forecasts for an event at time $t + h$, based on forecasts made at time t, $t + 1$, $t + 2$ and so on, the expert who obeys the LSN would systematically do worse than any regression-based model. Indeed, such a regression-based model would each time have a tendency to predict towards the mean of past observations, and systematic under- or over-prediction for the same horizon will not occur.

To highlight the LSN for experts, one can consider forecasts from models and experts when combined for the h-step-ahead horizon, where one needs multiple-steps-ahead forecasts. Combined model-based forecasts (CMF) for the same horizon can be written as

$$\text{CMF}_{t+h} = \sum_{j=0}^{h-1} \lambda_j \hat{y}_{t+h|t+j}$$

which is the weighted sum of h model-based forecasts for one and the same event at time h, and the combined expert forecast (CEF) is

$$\text{CEF}_{t+h} = \sum_{j=0}^{h-1} \lambda_j \hat{y}^E_{t+h|t+j},$$

which, similarly, is the weighted sum of expert-adjusted forecasts. The weights λ_j indicate the relative importance of the different forecasts. If experts' behaviour obeys the law of small numbers, the combined forecast CEF for horizon h is worse than the one-step-ahead forecast made at $h - 1$, while for the combined model-based forecast the success rate should be fifty–fifty.

Analysing 207 country/category combinations for the Organon database, the following results emerge upon application of the Clark and McCracken (2001) methodology (see also Chapter 4 below). Of the 207 country/category combinations the number of significantly better forecasts over just the model-based forecasts is counted. When using a binomial test, the 95 per cent confidence interval is then bounded by 89 and 118, or, in terms of fractions, 0.43 and 0.57. As mentioned, the managers at the Organon headquarters' office stated that the $h = 6$ horizon is important for reasons of supply chain management. Also, the bonus payments of local managers may in the end depend on their forecasts, predominantly for this horizon (although this idea was dismissed at a later stage, see the Preface).

The first set of results concerns the case where the weights λ_j are all equal to 1/6. Equal weights are often found to be best when combining forecasts (see Timmermann, 2006). For the combined model-based fore-casts the fraction of cases where CMF has a significantly better mean squared prediction error (MSPE) is 0.53. In contrast, for the combined expert forecasts CEF this fraction is only 0.41. Hence, the six averaged expert-adjusted forecasts for the same horizon are significantly worse than a one-step-ahead forecast based on the previous month. This shows that experts do not tend to redirect their forecasts back to some average level, whereas regression-model-based forecasts do that automatically. In other words, experts keep incorporating perceived recent exceptional observations too often for too long a period, and, at least for the Organon experts, the law of small numbers indeed seems to prevail.

Optimism

Another issue of expert-adjusted forecasts is whether adjustment brings the model forecasts closer to the realizations or whether the expert adjustment is in the wrong direction. The over-optimism bias as it is labelled in Fildes *et al.* (2009) would entail having more cases with $\hat{y}^E_{T+1|T} > \hat{y}_{T+1|T} > y_{T+1}$ than cases with $\hat{y}^E_{T+1|T} < \hat{y}_{T+1|T} < y_{T+1}$, that is, more cases where the expert's upward contribution brings the final forecasts further away from the truth instead of the other way around.

Table 1 of Franses and Legerstee (2011b) indicates that for one-step-ahead forecasts for the Organon database, the fraction of cases with $\hat{y}^E_{T+1|T} > \hat{y}_{T+1|T} > y_{T+1}$ is 22.9 per cent, while the fraction of cases with $\hat{y}^E_{T+1|T} < \hat{y}_{T+1|T} < y_{T+1}$ is 13.3 per cent. Optimism in the 'right' direction would mean that $\hat{y}_{T+1|T} < \hat{y}^E_{T+1|T} < y_{T+1}$, and this seems to occur in 16.8 per cent of cases. The same table shows that these num-bers are roughly constant across the forecast horizons 1 to 12. Hence, over-optimism occurs quite frequently.

WHAT DO EXPERTS THEMSELVES SAY THAT THEY DO?

The available Organon data concern forecasts made by experts in thirty-seven countries. Below some of their characteristics (like experience) will be incorporated to see if these have any predictive value, but first the survey results of Boulaksil and Franses (2009) will briefly be reviewed. Thanks to the efforts of senior staff at Organon, these authors were able to obtain the characteristics of the experts involved, such as age, gender and experience, and could send them a survey with various questions. Of all the experts involved (some countries have more than one), forty-two experts responded. The first key question was whether the experts actually considered the model-based forecasts as the input for their own forecasts. Quite surprisingly, no less than twenty-two of the forty-two respondents indicated that they do not consider these model forecasts at all, and that they somehow create their own forecasts.

For the twenty of the forty-two experts who said they did use the model-based forecasts as input, Boulaksil and Franses (2009) document that experts who first considered the model-based forecasts before they created their own final forecasts, (i) believed that a model-based forecast was important for their own decision to adjust, (ii) preferred to make small adjustments, (iii) did not believe that the model typically had the trend wrong, but (iv) were convinced that the model did not capture recent country-specific events. The latter is of course true, as the input of the FSS for Organon only included lagged sales data, hence rendering the forecast models pure time series models (like Holt–Winters, Box–Jenkins and combinations).

A second set of questions was answered by all forty-two experts. Experts who did not use the model-based forecasts as input for their adjustment felt that they could do just as well without those model forecasts and also that they used variables other than the model. Interestingly, those experts who did use the model forecasts saw no reason to have the model changed. Further, all experts seemed to include recent sales data as input for their adjustment. This could mean that the experts felt the model was not approximately adequate. This result concurs with the laboratory findings reported in Goodwin and Fildes (1999). There, people did not adjust the time series model forecast following a special event. In fact, when that happened they fully ignored the model-based forecast, and created their own forecast based on past data and somehow incorporated the effects of the special event. Based on the decision-making literature briefly addressed in Chapter 1, this practice will lead to sub-optimal forecasts.

Further survey outcomes were that the experts said they took account of changes in legislation and the local economy, and the behaviour of competitors in their specific countries, but not changes in the world economy. When recent sales figures fluctuated, the experts felt the need to adjust more. This is in accordance with the results from laboratory experiments in, for example, Harvey (1995). The experts stated that they felt quite confident about what they were doing. This seems to match the evidence obtained in Fildes and Goodwin (2007), which is that their experts did not mind much whether their adjustments actually improved their final expert-adjusted forecasts.

Finally, even though they felt confident, the Organon experts wanted to know more about how the model-based forecasts were actually created. This finding substantiates the often-heard claim that it is important that details on how forecasting support systems work should become available to their users; see also Gönül, Önkal and Lawrence (2006) and Yaniv and Kleinberger (2000).

DOES EXPERIENCE OR OTHER DESCRIPTIVES HAVE PREDICTIVE VALUE?

Using the data from Bayer, the large Leverkusen-based pharmaceutical company, De Bruijn and Franses (2012) operationalized the experience of the experts by the number of forecasts they had to make and the number of products that these forecasters were dealing with. On doing so the authors document that more experienced forecasters took past model-based forecast errors into account and they did so more than less experienced forecasters. Hence, there may seem to be some personal traits that can have predictive value for experts' adjustment behaviour.

A more detailed study on this aspect is provided in an earlier report in Legerstee and Franses (2007). A renewed analysis of their data is presented next. There is substantial relevant literature on the behaviour of experts who make forecasts (where no model forecasts are available) (see also an overview in Kahneman, 2012). For example,

Lamont (2002) examines forecast herding (that is, that forecasts of different experts are close to each other) and forecast scattering (the forecasts show dispersion) and the relation of herding and scattering with the professional lifetime of forecasters. Lamont (2002) considers published macroeconomic forecasts of numerous forecasters, and he concludes that as forecasters become older and more established (having a longer track record), they produce more radical and at the same time less accurate forecasts. It is suggested in Lamont (2002) that this is due to the fact that macroeconomic and financial forecasters have to build up a reputation and have to get media attention in order to stand out in a crowd of forecasters. Another cause of these less accurate forecasts could be cognitive decline due to aging (see Glisky, 2007). Recent evidence reported in Singh-Manoux et al. (2012) suggests that cognitive decline might already be setting in at around age forty-five. At the same time, it may also well be that younger forecasters produce more radical forecasts in order to attract attention.

Other relevant literature deals with ambiguity and gender differences in decision-making: see, for example, Powell and Ansic (1997), Eckel and Grossman (2008), Eriksson and Simpson (2010), and the recent survey by Croson and Gneezy (2009). The competence effect as it is put forward in Heath and Tversky (1991) is concerned with the phenomenon that people who perceive themselves as more competent are at the same time more willing to differ from others. In the present context this could mean that they would quote forecasts that more often deviate from model forecasts than others would do (see also Kliger and Levy, 2010), and hence that the size of the adjustment of the model-based forecasts increases. At the same time, forecasters who are more willing to differ from others may also consider multiple sources of information and may decide to average various available forecasts, and in that case they may deviate less from statistical model forecasts. Furthermore, Barber and Odean (2001), among others, document that male experts are apparently more over-confident than women.

There is a substantial literature on the effects of a person's own perceived competence and confidence on decision-making (see, for example, Heath and Tversky, 1991, among others), and part of the available evidence can be translated to the present situation of expert adjustment. When an expert is very competent, and thinks that he or she knows the local circumstances (economy, business) better than a statistical algorithm or econometric model could possibly do, he or she will quote forecasts that differ from model-based forecasts more and more often. In the words of Heath and Tversky (1991), he or she will be more willing to accept ambiguity. So, the size of the deviation will depend on the expert's own perceived competence.

Data on the Organon experts (see the Data Appendix Tables A2 to A4) contain the variables 'age' and 'years in position': that is, how long the local expert has been creating his or her own forecasts, and these are taken as proxies for competence. Note that the correlation between these two variables is likely to be non-zero, but not necessarily close to 1 as older individuals might just recently have been allocated a forecasting task. One could now conjecture that more experienced experts are more confident in their own capabilities and less confident in the adequacy and accuracy of the statistical model, and hence that more experienced experts give forecasts that differ from model forecasts more than less experienced experts would do.

Additional to the size of the adjustment, there is usually also information on the sign of the difference between the expert-adjusted forecast and the model forecast. This sign is of interest as it has been documented in Fildes *et al.* (2009) that upward adjustments of statistical forecasts can be more beneficial in terms of accuracy than downward adjustments, while Franses and Legerstee (2010) find the reverse outcome. Based on the econometric discourse in Chapter 2 there should, however, be no specific reason why this should be the case, at least on average, but perhaps various particular cases have particular outcomes. The model forecasts used by Organon are based on a statistical model fed by recent sales data, where such a statistical model typically has a tendency to converge to the mean value of the sales data, in particular when it comes to forecasting multiple steps ahead. The expert is responsible for the sales performance of his or her local unit. The risk function is perhaps asymmetric, as having too much stock is less harmful than having too little, simply because shipping takes time. Hence, underestimating sales might have stronger consequences for the local managers than overestimating future sales, and hence amounts to more risk to the manager. So one would expect that on average most experts would quote forecasts that exceed the model forecasts, and this is supported by the results in Fildes *et al.* (2009) and Franses and Legerstee (2009) (see also the beginning of this chapter). As more experience leads to a higher willingness to accept risk, this competence effect would imply that less experienced experts give forecasts that deviate from model forecasts more often upwards than downwards.

Finally, the decision-making and judgement literature also considers potential gender effects in decision-making and in accepting risk (see Croson and Gneezy, 2009 for a recent survey). A consistent finding in this literature is that women indicate preferences for less risky prospects and that they are less over-confident than men are: see Beyer and Bowden (1997) and some of the other references cited in Gysler, Kruse and Schubert (2002). Hence, male experts are more over-confident, and if so their forecasts would then deviate more from model forecasts than the forecasts of female experts, that is, the size of adjustment is larger.

To analyse whether any personal traits and other features associated with the expert forecaster have any link with the size and sign of expert adjustment, one can correlate these features in the Data Appendix with the properties of adjustment. The dataset with the forecasts is the same as that used in Franses and Legerstee (2009, 2010) and it is condensed for the present purposes. All relevant data appear in the Data Appendix.

Additional to the forecasts, there is information on the characteristics of the experts who create their forecasts, such as their age, gender and experience (measured by the number of products they cover), and the number of years that they are in a position to create the forecasts. At the same time, there is information on their forecast performance. The variable gender is coded as 0 for males and 1 for females. For some countries two experts are responsible for the forecasts, and then the average of the characteristics of the experts is taken. The countries are allocated across all continents, with most in Europe. Competence and experience are measured by age and years in position. In the Data Appendix there are some key statistics of these variables. It can be observed that the distribution of these explanatory variables reflects population features that were to be expected and the distributions are not strongly skewed towards certain outcomes. The correlation between age and years in position is 0.726.

To investigate to what extent the expert-adjusted forecasts differ from model-based forecasts, consider $D_{c,h,i} = \hat{y}^E_{c,h,i} - \hat{y}_{c,h,i}$ where $\hat{y}^E_{c,h,i}$ is the expert-adjusted forecast and $\hat{y}_{c,h,i}$ is the model-based forecast for country c, forecast horizon h (in months) and observation i. Consider the mean of the absolute deviations relative to the model-based forecast, calculated per country and per forecast horizon. This variable, to be labelled 'size of adjustment' is thus defined as

$$D_{c,h} = \frac{1}{n} \sum_i \frac{\text{abs}(D_{c,h,i})}{\hat{y}_{c,h,i}} \tag{3.8}$$

where n is shorthand for $n_{c,h}$, which is the number of observations for a country c and a horizon h. The subsequent analysis is confined to horizons $h = 1$ and $h = 6$, as these are the most relevant forecast horizons for the Organon experts.

The second variable to be explained, to be labelled 'sign of adjustment', is the number of upward adjustments as a percentage of all adjustments. It is calculated per country and per forecast horizon, that is,

$$pD_{c,h} = \frac{1}{n} \Sigma_i I(D_{c,h,i} > 0), \tag{3.9}$$

where $I(.)$ is an indicator function which takes the value 1 when its argument is true and zero otherwise. As I have said, the relevant data appear in Tables A3 and A4.

To investigate whether the characteristics of the experts are correlated with the experts' adjustments, two regression models are considered (each for one of the two horizons h). The first is

$$D_{c,h} = \mu + \beta_1 \log(\text{age}_c) + \beta_2 \log(\text{experience}_c) \\ + \beta_3 \log(\text{position}_c) + \beta_4 \text{gender}_c + \varepsilon_c \quad (3.10)$$

for $c = 1, 2, \ldots, 37$. For the variables 'sign of the adjustment' a logistic regression model is considered, which reads as

$$\log(pD_{c,h}/(1 - pD_{c,h})) = \mu + \beta_1 \log(\text{age}_c) + \beta_2 \log(\text{experience}_c) \\ + \beta_3 \log(\text{position}_c) + \beta_4 \text{gender}_c + \varepsilon_c \quad . \\ (3.11)$$

The parameters in both models can be estimated using OLS. For reasons of comparability the same variables in (3.11) as in (3.10) are included.

Table 3.5 shows that the size of expert adjustment cannot be reasonably explained by any of the observable characteristics of the experts. In contrast, Table 3.6 shows that older experts have an tendency to adjust more upwards, while more experienced experts adjust more often downwards. So, apparently competence (measured by age) and experience (measured by years in position) have contrasting effects on behaviour. Gender and years in position do not have any explanatory value.

In sum, and based on the Organon database, there seem to be no obvious traits and features of the expert forecasters that can convincingly explain their behaviour when adjusting model-based forecasts.

CONCLUSION

The empirical evidence, which is scattered throughout the literature, and also new evidence for previously never analysed data, has shown that there can be substantial differences between optimal behaviour (in an econometric sense) and the observed behaviour of experts adjusting model-based forecasts. There is some variation across the types of variables – that is, SKU-level sales for companies in the

Table 3.5: *Explanatory value of characteristics of experts for the size of expert adjustment (estimated standard error in parentheses)*

	Horizon	
Variable	$h = 1$	$h = 6$
Intercept	2.002 (1.694)	2.415 (2.008)
Log age	–0.174 (0.499)	–0.204 (0.576)
Log experience	–0.150 (0.131)	–0.165 (0.155)
Log position	0.097 (0.166)	0.044 (0.196)
Gender	0.336 (0.193)	0.287 (0.232)
Sample size	35	36
R^2	0.119	0.088
p-value of F-test	0.414	0.569
p-value of normality test	0.192	0.198

For size, $h = 1$, two observations are deleted (for countries 7 and 34), and for size, $h = 6$ the data for one expert (country 7) are not included. These observations caused the errors to be skewed and therefore they have been deleted.

pharmaceutical industry, airline revenues and key macroeconomic variables – but it seems possible to draw a few generalizing conclusions.

Chapter 2 suggested that an optimal setting for experts who provide adjustment to econometric model forecasts or forecasts from statistical algorithms would be that

Expert-Adjusted Forecast = Model Forecast + Adjustment

with the adjustment being unpredictable and orthogonal to the model forecast, where the model forecast obtains weight 1.

In this chapter it has been demonstrated that, in many practical situations, the adjustment is often not uncorrelated with the model forecast, and also that the deviation between the expert forecast and

Table 3.6: *Explanatory value of characteristics of experts for the fraction of upwards expert adjustment (estimated standard error in parentheses) (the 5 per cent significant parameters are in boldface and italics)*

Variable	Horizon	
	$h = 1$	$h = 6$
Intercept	-2.040 (1.278)	-1.788 (1.540)
Log age	***0.923 (0.355)***	***0.896 (0.436)***
Log experience	***-0.159 (0.098)***	***-0.215 (0.118)***
Log position	-0.013 (0.124)	0.040 (0.152)
Gender	-0.018 (0.143)	-0.047 (0.175)
Sample size	37	37
R^2	0.285	0.256
p-value of F-test	0.026	0.045
p-value of normality test	0.494	0.742

the model forecast can in various cases be predicted by a range of variables that are associated with past adjustment behaviour and past accuracy of expert-adjusted forecasts and model forecasts. Experts seem to be quite persistent in modifying model forecasts, and their behaviour seems to obey the law of small numbers, as predicted by the decision-making literature. Experts also have a preference for adjusting upwards. This behaviour could be a sign that experts misunderstand how the econometric models or forecast algorithms work, and perhaps more detailed explanations would reduce this. In Chapter 5 some potential evidence in this direction will be discussed. That experts adjust more often upwards can be associated with optimism bias, but perhaps also with the adoption of alternative loss functions. That is, the experts may find it difficult to disentangle their forecasting task from their management of shipments and stock. For macroeconomic forecasters it may be that revisions of national accounts data are also often upwards, and perhaps they already take such real-time data collection trends into account.

In contrast to the predictive content of past behaviour, experts' personal traits, such as experience, age and gender, do not seem to have much predictive value for the size and sign of the differences between expert-adjusted forecasts and model forecasts. Hence, to change experts' behaviour (and perhaps performance), managerial efforts should best address the current and past behaviour of experts instead of, say, replacing male by female experts. Hence, future adjustment behaviour seems to be associated more with what they have done and observed in the past than the individual traits of the experts. In other words, feedback on behaviour could help, and this will be discussed later on in Chapter 5.

Before looking at potential approaches to changing experts' adjustment behaviour, it is first important to see if any deviations from the optimal rule that the Expert Forecast = Model Forecast + Adjustment (and the associated optimal properties of the adjustment) make a difference in terms of forecast accuracy. The next chapter proceeds with this issue, where the accuracy of available expert-adjusted forecasts and model forecasts are compared, and where this observed accuracy is again linked with experts' adjustment behaviour.

4 How accurate are expert-adjusted forecasts?

The empirical evidence in the literature and some new results for new data, as reviewed in Chapter 3, show that the optimal situation (from an econometric perspective) as put forward in Chapter 2, that is,

Expert-Adjusted Forecast = Model Forecast + Adjustment,

where the adjustment has various specific properties, rarely seems to hold in practice. In fact, the observed differences between an available expert forecast and the associated model forecast seem predictable and are also more often positive than negative.

The literature provides a range of studies where the accuracy of expert-adjusted forecasts is compared with the accuracy of forecasts generated from econometric models or statistical algorithms. In this chapter a review of much of the currently available evidence is presented, where the earliest studies date back to the mid 1980s. The focus, however, is on recent evidence which is based on large databases. Also, as one might expect, these data allow for more generalizable results. It is important, though, to stress that only as early as Franses and Legerstee (2010) was methodology advocated to properly evaluate and compare the prediction quality, which takes account of the specific feature of expert-adjusted forecasts. Indeed, the key notion here is that when the expert-adjusted forecast is a function of the model forecast, the expert-adjusted forecast nests the model forecast. Hence, when comparing predictive accuracy, one has to take account of that nesting property.

A second notion that is outlined in more detail in this chapter is that it can happen that the model forecasts are not available to the analyst. In that case, the suggestion in Franses, McAleer and Legerstee (2009, 2014) can be followed, which is that the analyst creates his or her own econometric model based on publicly available data. The KLM case with the airline revenue data will be used to illustrate this approach.

EARLY EVIDENCE

Matthews and Diamantopoulos (1986) were among the first to analyse managerial intervention in forecasting in a real-life setting, when they actually had access to expert-adjusted forecasts and model-based forecasts. In those days there were some studies using experiments that found that judgemental adjustment reduced forecast accuracy, but for the first time these authors considered 281 actual forecasts for sales of repeat-purchase products from a company in the healthcare sector. In their Table 3, they report on five forecast accuracy measures, but for only two of these, that is, absolute error and percentage error, do they find significant differences in favour of what they call manipulated forecasts. In their Table 4 they report that the variance of the forecast error metrics is smaller for the manipulated forecasts in four of the five cases. Their Table 5 implements a regression of realizations on forecasts (as in equation (3.1)), and there it is found that for both the original and the manipulated forecasts there seems to be a bias: that is, the parameter associated with the forecast is significantly different from 1. Despite these findings, Mathews and Diamantopoulos (1986: 9) conclude that 'manipulation leads to an improvement in forecasting performance'. In their subsequent analysis of the same database, Diamantopoulos and Mathews (1989) document various factors that influence the forecast improvement of expert-adjusted forecasts, and they state that 'the greater the magnitude of revision, the greater the benefit in terms of forecast improvement' (1989: 57).

In their seminal paper on combining expert-adjusted forecasts with model-based forecasts, Blattberg and Hoch (1990) analyse the forecasts for five companies, where the samples with forecasts range from 100 to 1,008. Their Table 1 shows that in two of the five cases, the managers' (experts') forecasts are better, and something like 25 per cent of the variance left by the model seems to be picked up by the expert (manager).

For macroeconomic data, McNees (1990), Turner (1990) and Donihue (1993) address final expert forecasts for a variety of variables, where they specifically consider the quality of the expertise of the model-builders who can also exercise judgement during the model-building and forecast-creating stage. These authors all report that there are gains to be observed there too.

Since these early studies, the topic of expert adjustment has not been much studied, which is perhaps due to a lack of useful data. Also, given the developments in comparing predictive accuracy, initiated by Diebold and Mariano (1995), and readdressed after the important study of Clark and McCracken (2001) (and the many articles that have appeared since then), it may well be that the early methods may need slight modification. First, as was already noted in the previous chapter, before one can properly judge the quality of expert-adjusted forecasts and the potential driving factors of any empirical success, one needs to infer the properties of the model-based forecasts. Indeed, the model used in Mathews and Diamantopoulos (1986) seems to deliver biased forecasts (see Chapter 3), and hence one could perhaps expect, a priori, that expert-adjusted forecasts would deliver more accurate predictions. Second, as the expert-adjusted forecasts (can) encompass (nest) the model forecasts, it is recommended that the part associated with the model forecast is first stripped off. As reviewed in Chapter 2, it optimally holds that

Expert Forecast – Model Forecast = Adjustment

with some particular properties of adjustment, but the results in Chapter 3 show that there is more to be done than just analysing the difference between expert-adjusted forecasts and model forecasts. Indeed, perhaps only rarely is this difference an indicator of the relative contribution of the expert, as this assumes in advance that the weight of the model forecast in the expert-adjusted forecast is equal to 1, which is of course unknown from the outset.

To address this last issue directly, and also for illustrative purposes, consider the case where an analyst has only expert-adjusted
forecasts but no model forecasts, while the analyst is aware that the
expert somehow used the input of his or her own (or otherwise provided) model-based forecasts.

KLM

If an analyst wants to understand what causes the bias or success of
expert-adjusted forecasts, then the analyst somehow needs to make
assumptions about that expert forecast. Franses, McAleer and Legerstee
(2009) recommend assuming that the analyst has the ability to dissect
an expert forecast created at forecast origin $t - h$ for horizon t into what
they call a replicable part ($y^*_{t|t-h}$) and a non-replicable part e_t, that is,

$$\hat{y}^E_{t|t-h} = y^*_{t|t-h} + e_t. \tag{4.1}$$

The non-replicable part can be addressed as the latent (i.e. unobserved)
managerial adjustment, by approximation. The replicable part is the
part that the analyst can create, at least when he or she has econometric modelling skills. In fact, it is assumed that the replicable part can be
approximated by the conditional expectation based on the regression
model

$$y^*_{t|t-h} = W_{t-h-1}\delta + \varepsilon_t \tag{4.2}$$

where W_{t-h-1} contains all kinds of variables that are publicly known
to the analyst at time $t - h$, which is the origin at which the expert
makes the forecast, and where δ is a vector of parameters. Note that
this excludes information at time $t - h$ itself, and hence the additional
lag in W_{t-h-1}. The analyst can use (4.2) to approximate the replicable
part. Note that W_{t-h-1} also includes an intercept. Of course, the
analyst does not know exactly whether it was these variables that
could have been used by the expert, so again, (4.2) is only an
approximation.

The relevant test regression for forecast bias when using the
replicable forecast created by the analyst as in (3.1) now becomes

$$y_t = \alpha + \beta \hat{y}^*_{t|t-h} + u_t \tag{4.3}$$

where $\hat{y}^*_{t|t-h}$ follows from applying OLS to (4.2). As the regressor in (4.3) is a so-called generated regressor, one needs to use the Newey–West HAC standard errors.

To model the replicable part of the expert-adjusted forecast for KLM, the analyst (who in the present setting is the author of this book) decides to include in W_{t-h-1} an intercept and the following variables, that is, the harmonic regressors $\cos\frac{2\pi t}{12}$, $\sin\frac{2\pi t}{12}$, the exchange rate dollar versus euro (at time $t - h - 1$) ('Dollar/euro$_{t-h-1}$'), the natural log of the USA's industrial production index (at time $t - h - 1$) ('IP_USA$_{t-h-1}$'), the natural log of oil price (West Texas crude) (at time $t - h - 1$) ('Oil price$_{t-h-1}$') and unemployment rate in the USA (at time $t - h - 1$) ('Unemployment$_{t-h-1}$'), see also Franses (2013a). The OLS estimation results are given in Table 4.1, and the three models (one for each horizon) all have quite a large value of the R^2, meaning that a substantial fraction of the expert-adjusted forecast can be replicated. The harmonic regressors are relevant, but also the Wald tests for the joint significance of the other four economic variables (reported in the bottom row of the table) suggest that these also strongly contribute to the fit.

It may now be interesting to examine whether the forecast updates (from horizon 3 to 2 and from horizon 3 to 1) for the same fixed forecast event can also be replicated to some extent. For that purpose, one can regress $\log\hat{y}^E_{t|t-2} - \log\hat{y}^E_{t|t-3}$ on Dollar/euro$_{t-3}$, IP_USA$_{t-3}$, Oil price$_{t-3}$, and Unemployment$_{t-3}$ and on Dollar/euro$_{t-4}$, IP_USA$_{t-4}$, Oil price$_{t-4}$, and Unemployment$_{t-4}$. The R^2 of this regression is 0.308 and the F-test is 2.238 (p-value is 0.040). A regression of the most recent updates $\log\hat{y}^E_{t|t-1} - \log\hat{y}^E_{t|t-2}$ on the same variables and on Dollar/euro$_{t-2}$, IP_USA$_{t-2}$, Oil price$_{t-2}$, and Unemployment$_{t-2}$ gives an R^2 of 0.620 and an associated F-test of 5.037 (p-value is < 0.001). So it seems that the experts' updates of their own expert-adjusted forecasts can also be predicted by publicly available data.

Table 4.2 is concerned with the test regression (4.3), where the fit of the models in Table 4.1 is included. Clearly, the replicable

Table 4.1: *Modelling (the natural log of) the forecasts for total revenue data (Newey–West HAC standard errors in parentheses)*

Variable	Forecast horizon (in months)		
	3	2	1
Intercept	–1.077	–0.267	–6.334
	(4.567)	(4.431)	(2.841)
$\cos \dfrac{2\pi t}{12}$	–0.049	–0.053	–0.056
	(0.008)	(0.009)	(0.008)
$\sin \dfrac{2\pi t}{12}$	0.128	0.127	0.128
	(0.009)	(0.011)	(0.012)
Dollar/euro$_{t-h-1}$	0.096	0.056	–0.096
	(0.131)	(0.160)	(0.149)
IP_USA$_{t-h-1}$	1.466	1.273	2.604
	(0.984)	(0.974)	(0.635)
Oil price$_{t-h-1}$	0.041	0.074	0.024
	(0.052)	(0.064)	(0.064)
Unemployment$_{t-h-1}$	–0.049	–0.048	–0.001
	(0.045)	(0.041)	(0.026)
R^2	0.897	0.873	0.861
p-value (Wald test for all variables, except intercept and harmonic regressors)	0.000	0.000	0.000

Source: Table 2 in Franses (2013a).

components of the expert-adjusted forecasts are now found to be unbiased. Hence, here there is a case where the original expert-adjusted forecast, which is likely based on a model other than the one used by this analyst, is slightly biased (see Table 3.1), but the replicable forecast created by the analyst is not. This means that the analyst (and thus also the expert) could have come up with an unbiased forecast, and apparently it is the added managerial (expert) term that causes the bias.

Given that the available expert forecasts show bias, and the replicable component does not, would it be better to use only the latter model forecast? The results in Table 4.3 strongly suggest that this is

Table 4.2: *Testing for bias in replicable expert forecasts (total revenues) (Newey–West HAC standard errors in parentheses)*

Horizon	$\hat{\alpha}$	$\hat{\beta}$	Wald test (p-value)
Three months	0.264 (0.395)	0.955 (0.068)	0.446 (0.800)
Two months	0.206 (0.413)	0.965 (0.071)	0.252 (0.882)
One month	0.147 (0.361)	0.975 (0.061)	0.167 (0.920)

Test regression is:
$$\log y_t = \alpha + \beta \log \hat{y}^*_{t|t-h} + u_t$$
and the Wald test concerns the null hypothesis that $\alpha = 0$, $\beta = 1$. The model for the log of $\log y^*_{t|t-h}$ is presented in Table 4.1. In this regression, the fitted value is included as the explanatory variable. The sample size is 50, 53 and 55, for forecast horizons 3, 2 and 1, respectively.

Table 4.3: *Would an econometric model do better than the experts, based on root mean squared prediction error (total revenues)?*

Horizon	RMSPE		Improvement
	Model	Expert	
Three months	13.39	9.513	29%
Two months	11.57	8.659	23%
One month	13.88	6.661	52%

Source: Table 3 in Franses (2013a). The econometric model for horizon h is given in Table 4.1.

not the proper conclusion. The final expert-adjusted forecasts are much better than the model forecasts, in terms of root mean squared prediction error (RMSPE). So apparently the added non-replicable managerial intuition (or other insights) leading to an adjusted model-based forecast (not available to the analyst) certainly improves the forecast accuracy.

In sum, for total revenues the experts at KLM give much better forecasts than the analyst's model can replicate. This could be due to the possibility that the analyst did not include all the relevant variables. But then, still, the implemented econometric model does not give biased forecasts. Also, in times of downturn (around 2008) models kept on giving unbiased forecasts, in contrast to the expert-adjusted forecasts.

Pharmaceutical companies

For the Organon database Franses and Legerstee (2011b) document that the model forecasts are unbiased for all forecast horizons ranging from 1 to 12. The headquarters' office relies on an automated program, which, as mentioned, is a version of ForecastPro™. This statistical package creates monthly forecasts for one to twelve months ahead, and the statistical algorithm that generates these forecasts is updated each month. The program estimates the parameters of a variety of models and forecasting schemes, including the Box–Jenkins ARIMA type model, Holt–Winters extrapolation schemes and various combinations of them, and each month the best-performing model/algorithm is selected and forecasts are generated. This selection process is repeated each month, so it can occur that the previously best-performing model is replaced by another one, and vice versa. The input for all models is lagged sales data per specific product, up to and including lag 12. The experts are aware that the headquarters' office uses this forecast support system, but they do not have the opportunity to include their own personal input in the model. Later in Chapter 5 it will be seen whether that could have been beneficial.

Franses and Legerstee (2010) provide a systematic approach to evaluating the additional relevance of expert adjustment for forecast improvement. To discuss this method, consider again

$\hat{y}_{t+1|t}$: model-based one-step-ahead forecast (made from origin t)

$\hat{y}_{t+1|t}^{E}$: expert-adjusted one-step-ahead forecast (made from origin t)

y_{t+1}: realization at time $t + 1$.

The variable y denotes SKU-level sales here for the Organon data, and covers many products for many countries.

The model-based forecast usually amounts to an approximately linear function of past sales, where the weights are updated each month, thus providing a recursive forecasting scheme. One can thus write

$$\hat{y}_{t+1|t} = \mu_1 + \rho_1 y_t + \rho_2 y_{t-1} + \rho_3 y_{t-2} + \cdots \qquad (4.4)$$

The recursive scheme means that the parameters are estimated for R in-sample data, after which a one-step-ahead forecast is made. Next, the sample is increased to $R + 1$ in-sample data (while not dismissing the first observation) and the parameters are re-estimated and again a one-step-ahead forecast is made. The number of forecasts thus obtained is denoted as P.

The expert receives the statistical model-based forecasts and, as reviewed in Chapter 3, quite often makes an adjustment. In that chapter it was shown that part of that adjustment (the difference between the expert forecast and the model forecast) can be predicted from past sales and from other domain-specific variables, collected in, say, X_t containing, say, k_2 variables. Note that the inclusion of past sales in expert adjustment (perhaps because the expert feels that recent sales data are exceptional, and feels the need to keep on incorporating that information in future adjustments) implies that there is some form of double counting. This is because the recursive scheme for the model-based forecasts already allows for the additional impact of exceptional past sales data when updating the parameter estimates. In sum, the expert-adjusted forecast might now be approximated by

$$\hat{y}_{t+1|t}^E = \mu_2 + \delta_1 y_t + \delta_2 y_{t-1} + \delta_3 y_{t-2} + \cdots + \beta X_t + \cdots \qquad (4.5)$$

As the expert usually does not write down how he or she modified the model-based forecast, there is no specific information on X_t. Comparing (4.5) with (4.4) shows that the forecasting scheme of the expert nests the forecasting scheme of the model, as (4.5) contains the same variables as (4.4) and more. If one were to call (4.5) the 'model' used by the expert, then model (4.5) is said to nest model (4.4). This observation is important as it has implications for the statistical methodology to be used below for testing whether (4.5) is significantly better than (4.4) in terms of forecast accuracy.

There are two ways of defining the added contribution of the expert to the model-based forecast. The first is simply assuming that adjustment equals $\hat{y}^E_{T+1|T} - \hat{y}_{T+1|T}$, which already assumes that the adjustment and the model forecast are independent and that the expert takes the model-based forecasts as given by assigning a weight 1, and adding his or her adjustment, as it should be according to Chapter 2. The second way amounts to computing

$$A_{t+1|t} = \hat{y}^E_{t+1|t} - \lambda\hat{y}_{t+1|t} \tag{4.6}$$

where λ is estimated from a linear regression, as recommended in Blattberg and Hoch (1990). In what follows (4.6) will be used, simply because the value of λ is unknown in advance.

The first question that needs to be answered when comparing expert-adjusted forecasts and model-based forecasts is whether the added value of the expert actually matters (which can be either in a positive or a negative way); that is, does the adjustment add any information to the available model-based forecast? This question can be answered by considering the following auxiliary test regression

$$y_{t+1} = \alpha + \beta\hat{y}_{t+1|t} + \gamma A_{t+1|t} + u_{t+1} \tag{4.7}$$

where $A_{t+1|t}$ follows from (4.6) after estimating λ. When the expert adds something that is relevant to forecast the one-step-ahead observation, additional to the model-based forecast, the contribution of $A_{t+1|t}$ in (4.7) should be non-zero. Hence, a first potentially interesting test concerns examining whether $\gamma = 0$ in (4.7).

A second question that is of interest is whether the contribution of the model-based forecast and that of the expert-adjusted forecast are somehow in balance: that is, does the 50 per cent model/50 per cent manager (expert) rule (as advocated in Blattberg and Hoch, 1990) hold? It should be stressed here that one may wonder whether this 50 per cent/ 50 per cent rule should concern the forecast of the manager $\hat{y}^E_{t+1|t}$

or the added value $A_{(t+1|t)}$ of the manager. Quite conceivably it should be the added value, and this then makes (4.7) the proper equation to consider. Indeed, if instead one were to consider the auxiliary test regression

$$y_{t+1} = \alpha + \beta \hat{y}_{t+1|t} + \theta \hat{y}^E_{t+1|t} + u_{t+1}, \tag{4.8}$$

one should be aware that given (4.6) this implies

$$y_{t+1} = \alpha + (\beta + \theta\lambda)\hat{y}_{t+1|t} + \theta A_{t+1|t} + u_{t+1}. \tag{4.9}$$

In other words, if one were to find a 50 per cent/50 per cent balance between $\hat{y}^E_{t+1|t}$ and $\hat{y}_{t+1|t}$ using model (4.8), then this would not tell us anything about the balance between $A_{t+1|t}$ and $\hat{y}_{t+1|t}$, as this depends on the value of λ, which has to be estimated too. So, one should preferably be looking directly at (4.7) and, based on this test regression, one can examine the second interesting hypothesis that $\beta = \gamma$ in (4.7), meaning that the added contribution of the expert is equally important as the model-based forecast.

Is the RMSPE of the expert forecast significantly lower than that of the model forecast?

To test the null hypothesis that the RMSPE, across a number of cases of the expert forecast is equal to that of the model forecast, against the alternative hypothesis that the expert delivers more accurate expert-adjusted forecasts, one needs to take account of the fact that model (4.5) nests model (4.4), at least from an econometric perspective. As is convincingly explained in Clark and McCracken (2001), due to this nesting property the relevant test statistic based on suggestions in Diebold and Mariano (1995) does not have a standard (here, normal) distribution.

Following the recommendation in Clark and McCracken (2001), the following procedure will therefore be considered. As mentioned, for the Organon case there are R in-sample data, where, as far as is known to the author of this monograph, R concerns five years of monthly data, so $R = 60$. There are P recursively created out-of-sample one-step-ahead forecasts, with here $P = 25$. Hence, the fraction of forecasts over the number of in-sample data is

$$\pi = \frac{P}{R} \approx 0.4.$$

This value of π is needed for the non-standard critical values of the upcoming test.

As I have said, model (4.5) nests model (4.4). It is usually not known how many variables are included in the additional set of regressors X_t, but for convenience that number k_2 is set here equal to 2. This value amounts to a guess as it assumes that experts, on average, have another two variables in mind when creating their expert-adjusted forecasts. Based on simulations concerning empirical size and power, Clark and McCracken (2001) recommend using the so-called ENC-NEW test (where ENC means 'encompassing'), defined by

$$\text{ENC-NEW} = P \frac{\frac{1}{P}\sum \left(u_{1,t+1}^2 - u_{1,t+1}u_{2,t+1} \right)}{\frac{1}{P}\sum u_{2,t+1}^2} \tag{4.10}$$

The summation runs for the P one-step-ahead forecasts, and $u_{1,t+1}$ denotes the forecast errors for model-based forecasts (equation (4.4)), and $u_{2,t+1}$ concerns the expert-adjusted forecasts (equation (4.5), which nests scheme (4.4)). The 5 per cent critical values are given in Table 1 of Clark–McCracken (2001: 92). For $\pi = 0.4$ and $k_2 = 2$ the critical value is 1.481. Note that this test is a one-sided test of the null hypothesis that model (4.5) performs equally well as model (4.4) against the alternative hypothesis that model (4.5) provides more accurate forecasts. So the aim of the test is whether the expert-adjusted forecasts provide significantly more accuracy than plain model-based forecasts or not.

Multiple-steps-ahead forecasts

When there is an interest in examining whether experts do better than models when it comes to h-steps-ahead forecasts, one can consider the variables

$\hat{y}_{t+h|t}$: model-based forecast (made from origin t)

$\hat{y}^E_{t+h|t}$: expert-adjusted forecast (made from origin t)

y_{t+h}: realization at $t + h$.

As in the case of one-step-ahead forecasts, one can consider the auxiliary test regression

$$y_{t+h} = \alpha + \beta \hat{y}_{t+h|t} + \gamma A_{t+h|t} + u_{t+h}, \tag{4.11}$$

Where the adjustment is defined as before and tests the hypotheses that $\gamma = 0$ and, if it is not, whether $\beta = \gamma$.

One can also compute a test statistic as in (4.10), but now a complication arises in terms of the asymptotic distribution of that test. For multiple-steps-ahead forecasts it is well known that the forecast errors are correlated, and this correlation needs to be included in the distribution. Clark and McCracken (2005) outline in detail how to do this in case the variables in X_t are known. One can then use bootstrap techniques to compute critical values for each particular situation. In the present case there is the problem that these variables, which are the additional variables used by the expert, are unknown. Fortunately, Clark and McCracken (2005: 390) note that standard normal critical values would lead to reliable inference, at least provided that the forecast horizon is relatively short and that π is also quite small. As this corresponds with the Organon configurations, one can therefore rely on the statistic

$$\text{ENC-NEW}_h = P \frac{\frac{1}{P} \sum \left(u^2_{1,t+h} - u_{1,t+h} u_{2,t+h} \right)}{\frac{1}{P} \sum u^2_{2,t+h}} \tag{4.12}$$

which again will be considered as a one-sided test, now with a 5 per cent critical value equal to 1.645.

To be able to use these test statistics, Franses and Legerstee (2010) summarize the Organon data into 194 cases which involve the data for countries (out of the 37) and product categories (out of the 7). As $7 \times 37 = 259$, it is clear that there are not sufficient data for all countries and categories, and this means that the various results are not always based on the same number of cases. And as the sample size concerns twenty-five monthly observations, the test outcomes are pooled across the data in each of the 194 cases. Table II in Franses and Legerstee (2010) shows that for 53.6 per cent of the 194 cases the added contribution of the expert-adjusted forecast (the part $A_{t+1|t}$) is significant at the 5 per cent level. The estimate of β is on average 0.27, while γ is on average estimated as equal to 0.25. In 60.8 per cent of the cases the differences between these two parameters are not different from 0. Finally, on average λ is estimated equal to 0.4.

Using (4.10), Franses and Legerstee (2010) further document that, when the RMSPEs are significantly different, the improvement of expert-adjusted forecasts over model-based forecasts is 14.4 per cent. At the same time, when the differences are not significant, such improvement is –13.8 per cent. This suggests that if expert-adjusted forecasts are more accurate, they are just a little bit more accurate than when the forecasts are not different (meaning, in many cases, worse, as one should recall that the test is one-sided). Hence, in an absolute sense, this seems to suggest that expert-adjusted forecasts do not lead to much more accuracy.

With β and γ in (4.7) about equally large, this means that the relative weights of $\hat{y}^E_{t+1|t}$ and $\hat{y}_{t+1|t}$ according to (4.9) are close to 0.625 and 0.375, respectively, given the average value of λ. Franses and Legerstee (2010) conclude their study with an examination of whether the weights 0.5 and 0.5 instead of 0.625 and 0.375 would have led to more accurate forecasts. Given that λ is found to be equal to 0.4, on average, these 50 per cent/50 per cent weights would assign less value to the experts' deviation from the model forecasts and more to the model forecasts. With these new weights, the average RMSPE across the 194 cases now becomes 5.47 per cent, where it was originally –10.18 per cent. So it seems that alternative weights do appear to lead to more forecast accuracy. This issue will be addressed further in Chapter 5.

De Bruijn and Franses (2012), who consider a very large database concerning sales and forecasts for the products of Bayer, the German pharmaceutical company, report results for the natural logarithm of the median of the absolute percentage error per product. These authors use this measure in particular in order to compare products and volumes, and also because their data involve a number of extreme-valued observations. Using latent class modelling, the authors find evidence that there are two types of forecasters, who differ in their behaviour and experience. The average values of the median-based error measures are 1.162 and 0.736 for the expert-adjusted forecasts and 0.969 and 0.630 for the model-based forecasts. This means that, on average, the percentage deterioration of the expert-adjusted forecasts is 19.9 per cent and 16.8 per cent, respectively. These numbers are in accordance with the numbers in Franses and Legerstee (2010) for different data (country, products and time). Hence, there seems to be a persistent outcome here.

DOES THE FORECAST HORIZON MATTER?

Franses and Legerstee (2011a) consider (4.11) and (4.12) for horizons 1 to 12 for the Organon data. Due to a lack of data, the number of cases for each horizon is not constant and varies in a range from 203 to 185. After correcting for potential loss of power of the test statistics due to smaller amounts of data, the authors conclude that the added value of expert adjustment is significant in approximately 50 per cent of the cases, across all horizons. The fraction of cases with β equal to γ while γ is different from 0 reduces from 51.4 per cent of the cases for horizon 1 to 30.4 per cent of the cases for horizon 12, although there is some peak around horizon 6, which is the horizon that is now known to be most relevant to the Organon managers. This is partly in contrast to the expectations in Chapter 2 that experts would find it more difficult to sensibly contribute for more distant horizons.

Considering the RMSPE and also the mean absolute percentage error (MAPE), Table 4 in Franses and Legerstee (2011a) shows that expert-adjusted forecasts are on average less accurate than model-based forecasts. The peak in this loss of accuracy is again observed for horizon 6, which leads the authors to suggest that a larger weight of experts' adjustment (based on intuition or their own models) matches with less accuracy. Also their Table A1 shows that the average absolute percentage difference between expert-adjusted forecasts and model-based forecasts is largest around horizon 6. Relying on the test in (4.12), their Table 5 indicates that when expert-adjusted forecasts are better, they are more so for more distant horizons. In turn, this also translates to the 50 per cent/50 per cent combinations, as discussed before, where these combinations again yield more improvement for more distant horizons.

FACTORS THAT AFFECT FORECAST ACCURACY

With their first in-depth study on expert-adjusted forecasts, albeit considering just 281 forecasts, Diamantopoulos and Mathews (1989) concluded that it was the larger deviations from model forecasts that provided better accuracy. This finding is reiterated in Fildes *et al.* (2009) who conclude that 'relatively larger adjustments tended to lead to greater average improvements in accuracy' (2009: 3), while at the same time 'smaller adjustments often damaged accuracy' (2009: 3). Considering again the theoretical arguments in Chapter 2, it seems that the beneficial effect of large adjustments could be due to model forecasts which were biased in the first place, as strictly speaking from an econometric point of view there is no reason to expect that larger adjustments would lead to more accuracy than small adjustments. Indeed, and as noted before, Mathews and Diamantopoulos (1986) document that their model forecasts show strong bias. Whether the model-based forecasts used in Fildes *et al.* (2009) show bias is unknown, at least to this author.

Concerning the sign of expert adjustment, Fildes *et al.* (2009) provide clear-cut evidence. Positive adjustments are found less likely to improve accuracy than negative deviations from model forecasts. Also, such positive deviations were also quite often in the wrong direction. Again, based on the material in Chapter 2, if the model-based forecasts are unbiased, there is no reason to believe that either merely upwards or downwards adjustments would lead to more accuracy. Of course, in individual cases one could observe that a few more positive adjustments than negative ones lead to more accuracy, but on average across many cases these should cancel out, at least in the optimal situation (in an econometric sense).

In fact, one would suspect, while assuming that the model-based forecasts are unbiased, that large and persistent deviations from model forecasts could be harmful and also that an unbalanced distribution of the signs of the deviations would on average also lead to less accuracy. Indeed, De Bruijn and Franses (2012), who have analysed the huge Bayer database, concluded that 'smaller deviations from Forecast Support System (FSS) forecasts and less optimistic adjustments lead to better forecasts' (2012: 19). At the same time, Franses and Legerstee (2010) conclude for the Organon database that 'experts deviate too much from the model forecasts. When we downplay the modification of the expert, we see strong improvement in final forecast quality' (2012: 339).

Legerstee, Franses and Paap (2011), while introducing a new two-level hierarchical Bayes model to link forecast accuracy with expert behaviour, draw a few further conclusions. The first is that experts, when creating their forecasts, which are possibly based on available model forecasts, take factors into account which also influence the model-based forecasts. Bunn and Salo (1996) called this phenomenon 'double counting', and it reflects the expressions in (4.4) and (4.5). When experts do this, the error term in the regression of the expert-adjusted forecast on the model-based forecast is correlated with the model-based forecast. In econometric language this means that the model forecasts are endogenous in the regression model. Legerstee, Franses and Paap (2011) show that the larger the correlation between errors and model forecasts the lower the accuracy of the expert-adjusted forecasts. A second conclusion in their study is that experts who stick close to the original model-based forecasts in general show most accuracy in their expert-adjusted forecasts. These findings substantiate the theoretical results in Chapter 2.

Personal traits, again

When analysing the percentage improvement of expert-adjusted fore-casts over model-based forecasts, one can also examine whether any of the experts' personal traits matter. For example, do factors like gender and age matter? Table 4.4 provides some insights concerning the thirty-seven experts at Organon. Column 2 concerns the results for the one-step-ahead horizon. It is evident that not much variance in the percentage improvement is explained, and that only the log of experi-ence (now measured by the number of products that an individual expert has to deal with) has a significant positive effect. That is, more experience leads to more accurate expert-adjusted forecasts. For the six-months-ahead forecasts, this variable again has a significant

Table 4.4: *Potential factors driving the improvement in expert-adjusted forecasts over model forecasts (estimated standard errors in parentheses). Boldface italic denotes parameters significant at the 5 per cent level*

	Horizon 1	Horizon 6*
Intercept	−2.780 (75.09)	10.75 (31.17)
Log of age	−18.64 (21.49)	*−20.97 (9.265)*
Log of experience	*13.70 (5.652)*	*6.075 (2.535)*
Log of years in position	−1.855 (6.979)	2.165 (2.844)
Gender	−6.300 (8.528)	2.397 (3.396)
Size of expert-adjustment	1.212 (2.452)	*−1.627 (0.420)*
Fraction of positive adjustments	−44.55 (43.78)	32.01 (17.09)
R^2	0.285	0.616
p-value of F-test	0.123	< 0.001
p-value test for normality test	0.152	0.942

* Observations 8, 22 and 37 have been deleted as they are outliers.

positive effect (see column 3 of Table 4.4). Additionally, older experts provide less accuracy, and larger deviations from the model forecasts lead to less accuracy. The sign of the expert adjustment is not significant at the 5 per cent level.

CPB

Based on the many forecasts available for pharmaceutical companies, it seems that expert-adjusted forecasts that are close to the model-based forecasts, and which do not have a particular tendency to move either upwards or downwards, seem to provide the highest accuracy. It would now be interesting to see if these findings also hold for the macroeconomic forecasts, used as a running example throughout this monograph. Table 13 of Franses, Kranendonk and Lanser (2011) presents the results of regression (4.8). There are eighty cases (four forecast origins, two types of macroeconomic data, that is, first release and final release, and ten variables), and only twenty-two cases show significant contributions of the expert-adjusted forecasts in regression (4.8). Tables 11 and 12 of that same study show that forecast errors of expert-adjusted forecasts are smaller, in particular for the price variables, but also for the volumes of consumption and investments.

Whether these improvements are due to the specific behaviour of experts is not presented in Franses, Kranendonk and Lanser (2011), and will be discussed next. For this purpose a new set of forecasts is analysed and these concern annual data from 1990 to 2007 (drawn from Kranendonk and Verbruggen, 2007). These data concern the forecasts for thirteen macroeconomic variables for year T, when these forecasts are made in the spring of year $T-1$ (to be called horizon 4), in the autumn of year $T-1$ (horizon 3), in the spring of year T (horizon 2) and in the autumn of year T (horizon 1). It is now of interest to see whether there is any improvement in the forecasts for the same fixed event, and whether such improvement could be due to the manual touch of the CPB experts.

Table 4.5 reports on the percentage improvement of more recent forecasts (horizons 3, 2 and 1) using the measure (expressed as a percentage):

Table 4.5: *Improvement of forecast updates (relative to horizon 4) for the same event using the measure (4.13)*

Variable	Horizon = 1	Horizon = 2	Horizon = 3
GDP, volume	0.72	0.46	0.07
Consumption	0.88	0.69	0.18
Wages	0.98	0.97	0.32
CPI	0.96	0.88	0.30
Export, price	0.89	0.70	−0.01
Export, volume	0.77	0.65	0.01
Import, price	0.91	0.60	0.03
Import, volume	0.76	0.56	0.08
Investments	0.62	0.53	0.06
GDP, price	0.87	0.91	0.36
Employment	0.82	0.62	−0.12
World trade, price	0.90	0.62	−0.29
World trade, volume	0.72	0.51	0.09
Average	0.83	0.67	0.08

$$1 - \frac{\text{MSPE}_{h=h}}{\text{MSPE}_{h=4}} \qquad (4.13)$$

where MSPE denotes the mean squared prediction error. On average, the improvement from horizon 4 to horizon 1 turns out to be 83 per cent. This improvement seems to hold for almost all variables, where most improvement can be noticed for wages (98 per cent) and the consumer prices index (CPI) (96 per cent).

Table 4.6 refers to the percentage improvement of forecasts for horizon h versus horizon $h - 1$ using the measure (as a percentage)

$$1 - \frac{\text{MSPE}_{h-1}}{\text{MSPE}_h}. \qquad (4.14)$$

Table 4.6: *Improvement of forecast updates for the same event using the measure (4.14). (The non-significant improvements according to the ENC-NEW test of Clark and McCracken (2001) are in italic and boldface*

Variable	Horizon		
	1 versus 2	2 versus 3	3 versus 4
GDP, volume	0.48	0.42	*0.07*
Consumption	0.61	0.62	0.18
Wages	0.33	0.96	0.32
CPI	0.67	0.83	0.30
Export, price	0.63	0.70	*-0.01*
Export, volume	0.34	0.65	*0.01*
Import, price	0.78	0.59	*0.03*
Import, volume	0.45	0.52	*0.08*
Investments	0.19	0.50	*0.06*
GDP, price	*-0.44*	0.86	0.36
Employment	0.53	0.66	*-0.12*
World trade, price	0.74	0.71	*-0.29*
World trade, volume	0.43	0.46	*0.09*
Average	0.44	0.65	0.08

The average improvement is largest from horizon 3 to 2, with an average value of 65 per cent. With newly simulated critical values (available from the author upon request), the ENC-NEW test from Clark and McCracken (2001) gives significant improvements for horizons 3 to 2 and for 2 to 1.

Table 4.7 gives the percentage improvements for the ten variables that were also analysed in Franes, Kranendonk and Lanser (2011), and the mean of the size of the adjustments (2011: Table 1, column Q3) for the improvement for horizon 4 to 3. Figure 4.1 shows that there is a clear positive relation between the two, although investments (to the

Table 4.7: *The data for improvement and mean adjustment*

	Improvement	Adjustment
GDP, volume	0.07	0.20
Consumption	0.18	0.38
Wages	0.32	0.83
CPI	0.30	0.55
Export, price	-0.01	0.08
Export, volume	0.01	-0.09
Import, volume	0.08	0.14
Investments	0.06	1.50
GDP, price	0.36	0.52
Employment	-0.12	-0.16

Source: Franses, Kranendonk and Lanser (2011: Table 1, column Q3).

right-hand side of the graph) may be an outlier. A regression of the variable improvement on an intercept and mean adjustment gives an estimate of 0.148 (estimated HAC standard error is 0.122) for mean adjustment and an R^2 of 0.212. Deleting the observation for investment, the parameter is estimated as 0.483 (0.077) and the R^2 increases to 0.877.

In sum, for the CPB data it seems that expert manipulation of the model-based forecasts does lead to significant improvement in forecast updates. At the same time, such improvement does not seem to be associated with only positive or only negative adjustments.

CONCLUSION

This chapter has presented the empirical evidence from a range of recent studies, some of which have been published in the recent academic literature, while other evidence was new. One finding is that, in particular cases, expert adjustment can lead to forecasts which are more accurate than model-based forecasts. When these model-based forecasts are biased, experts may generate substantial improvement,

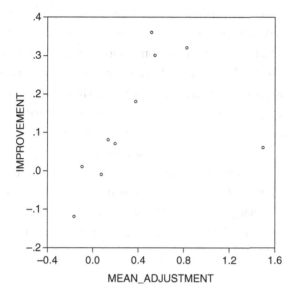

FIGURE 4.1. Improvement in forecast accuracy for horizon 4 to horizon 3 versus mean of the expert adjustment of forecasts (the data are presented in Table 4.7).

and then larger adjustments can also be beneficial. However, when considering a large number of expert-adjusted forecasts and looking at results across many cases, it appears that currently available and empirically observed expert-adjusted forecasts are not doing very well, perhaps because they deviate too much from the model-based forecasts.

When model-based forecasts are unbiased, and this seems to be (or should be) a common situation, and because the analyst can create an unbiased forecast based on publicly available data, it seems that irregular, evenly signed, and not too large and extravagant adjustments lead to the most incremental accuracy. This matches the notion in Chapter 2 that, optimally, an expert-adjusted forecast is equal to a model-based forecast plus some adjustment where optimal adjustment obeys a few important rules. Deviations from this rule apparently lead to less accuracy, as is documented in a range of settings demonstrated in this chapter. Personal experience with forecasting does improve the accuracy of expert-adjusted forecasts and also younger experts tend to perform better, but useful evidence on personal traits is limited. It seems that the past adjustment behaviour of experts matters most, and in light of this behaviour one may find ways to modify behaviour to improve forecast accuracy. One cannot change people's expertise or gender, but one might perhaps be able to change experts' behaviour.

As deviations from the optimal rule (in an econometric sense) seem to be prevalent in practice, one might want to find ways to make experts adhere to that rule. At the same time, in case experts do not and are not willing to change their behaviour, what could make forecasts for the end-user even better? These issues will be addressed in Chapter 5.

5   How can forecasts be improved?

The current state of affairs concerning experts adjusting model-based forecasts is summarized in the previous two chapters. Chapter 3 showed that experts adjust model-based forecasts very frequently, whether the data concern business or economic variables, and perhaps more often than is really necessary, at least from an econometric perspective outlined in Chapter 2. Such adjustments by experts can be large in size, and this might perhaps be associated with biased model-based forecasts. Indeed, even the elaborate CPB macroeconomic model seems to deliver biased forecasts for various important macroeconomic variables. It was also found that expert adjustment is more often upwards than downwards, which may be a sign of (over-) optimism, or perhaps of alternative loss functions, as will be discussed in the present chapter. In individual cases it can be that more upwards than downwards adjustment may be a useful strategy, but on average, across many cases, there is no need (at least econometrically) to have more upward than downward adjustments.

The empirical results summarized in Chapter 4 showed that the apparent downside of the tendency to frequently modify model forecasts seems to be that the scrutinized expert-adjusted forecasts currently available are not very much better than the model forecasts, at least on average. Again, in individual cases it can occur that expert adjustment leads to substantial forecast improvement, but on average current insights suggest that expert adjustment as it is carried out now is not very useful. It seems in fact that when expert-adjusted forecasts are better they are only a little better, and when they are worse, they are much worse. For the CPB forecasts we learn that when experts really do have expertise concerning a certain variable, their added value can lead to substantial improvements. On the other hand, for the pharmaceutical sales forecasts we learn that most experts seem to be inclined to deviate too much from the model forecasts, which on average leads to no improvement.

In Chapter 2 it has been argued that it would be optimal if

Expert-Adjusted Forecast = Model Forecast + Adjustment

with the model forecast having weight 1, and where the adjustment is an unpredictable variable which only once in a while takes a non-zero value, and which is orthogonal to (or uncorrelated with) the model forecast. From Chapters 3 and 4 it became clear, however, that in many situations it seems to hold that

Expert-Adjusted Forecast = α Model Forecast + β Contribution
of Expert

with

$\beta \gg \alpha$.

In fact, it was also documented that the smaller α is relative to β, the worse the accuracy of the expert-adjusted forecasts seems to become. Below it will be demonstrated that α can be allowed to be smaller than 1, as long as this is associated with the situation where Expert-Adjusted Forecast $- \alpha \times$ the Model Forecast is predictable using publicly available data, which entails that the experts may have used input variables other than the ones used for the model forecast. In other words, the less prominent the adjustment or the contribution of the expert that cannot be replicated by an analyst, the better the expert-adjusted forecasts become.

While having documented in Chapter 4 that apparently the expert-adjusted forecasts can somehow be improved, this chapter deals with two strategies for how such improvements might be carried out. The first is that experts could have relied on an alternative loss function, and perhaps this should be changed. Such a change in behaviour should be easy to establish. The second strategy amounts to providing feedback with the hope that this can make experts change their behaviour. As will be seen, feedback can indeed help. One type of feedback is simply to show experts what the consequences of their behaviour are. Another type, which could be carried out in future research, is to make experts write down what and why they actually did what they did. This follows the suggestions of Goodwin (2000), among others. At present not much empirical data is available on this strategy, so no conclusions can yet be drawn.

Alternatively, it may also be that model forecasts can be improved, and in such a way that experts feel less inclined to modify them. One way to do this is to incorporate past expert adjustment into the model, as it could well be that such past adjustment carries relevant information. The first results for this approach seem positive, although general statements should await more empirical results.

Finally, for the end-user of forecasts it can also be a good idea to combine expert-adjusted forecasts and model forecasts. This chapter concludes with the latter notion and shows that salient benefits can indeed be gained.

IMPROVING EXPERT FORECASTS

One possible reason why experts may quote forecasts that more often deviate upwards from model forecasts is that the experts have other loss functions in mind when they create their own forecasts. The loss function underlying model forecasts and many statistical algorithms is the mean squared error loss function. Strictly speaking, when adjusting model forecasts, experts can stick to the same loss function, but maybe they do not.

Alternatively, it may be that experts are perhaps not aware of how much they deviate on average, and what the consequences are in terms of forecast accuracy. Perhaps feedback on their actual behaviour and performance may bring about a change.

Do experts use another loss function?

The standard linear regression model entails the assumption of a quadratic loss function when estimating the parameters. Indeed, the popular estimation method of ordinary least squares (and many of its variants) involves minimizing the sum of squares of deviations from the model fit with the actual data. One may, however, decide to consider alternative loss functions when calibrating the model and constructing forecasts; see Christoffersen and Diebold (1996, 1997) and Zellner (1986) for some early references. For one-step-ahead forecasts, the often-applied squared loss function can be written as

$$Q(y_{t+1}, \hat{y}_{t+1|t}) = (\hat{y}_{t+1|t} - y_{t+1})^2. \tag{5.1}$$

This loss function penalizes over-prediction and under-prediction equally, which in many situations seems to be reasonable. It may, however, be that one wishes to penalize under-prediction more than over-prediction, perhaps because one feels that being out-of-stock is considered worse than having too much stock (which could indeed be the case for the pharmaceutical sales forecasters). The so-called lin-lin loss function can then be useful and it is given by

$$LL(y_{t+1}, \hat{y}_{t+1|t}) = \alpha|\hat{y}_{t+1|t} - y_{t+1}| \ \text{if} \ \hat{y}_{t+1|t} < y_{t+1} \tag{5.2}$$

and

$$LL(y_{t+1}, \hat{y}_{t+1|t}) = |\hat{y}_{t+1|t} - y_{t+1}| \ \text{if} \ \hat{y}_{t+1|t} > y_{t+1}. \tag{5.3}$$

When it holds that $\alpha > 1$, under-prediction is penalized more than over-prediction; see Ferguson (1967). Another asymmetric loss function which can be useful is the so-called linex loss function proposed in Varian (1975) and Zellner (1986). This function is given by

$$LIN(y_{t+1}, \hat{y}_{t+1|t}) = \exp(\beta(\hat{y}_{t+1|t} - y_{t+1})) - \beta(\hat{y}_{t+1|t} - y_{t+1}) - 1. \tag{5.4}$$

When it holds that $\beta < 0$, under-prediction is penalized more than over-prediction. Elliott, Komunjer and Timmermann (2005) propose a method for selecting a loss function. Franses, Legerstee and Paap (2011) propose an alternative method that is particularly useful for the Organon case as it exploits the fact that forecasts are available for many individual experts, and that the associated model-based forecasts are available too. The latter allows for an easy-to-perform check if the model forecasts are based on the quadratic loss function in (5.1).

The application of the second method mentioned leads to the following results for the Organon experts and their expert-adjusted forecasts. For the lin-lin loss function, α is estimated as significantly different (at the 5 per cent level) from 1 in twenty-two of the thirty-five cases. Note that the number of cases is smaller than before due to data availability. On average the α parameter is estimated to be equal to 1.40, meaning for the Organon expert-adjusted forecasts that under-prediction gets a 40 per cent larger penalty than over-prediction, which corresponds to expectations. Using the linex loss function, the parameter β in (5.4) is estimated to be significantly smaller than 0 in fifteen of the thirty-five cases. An application of the Elliott, Komunjer and Timmermann (2005) method reveals similar kinds of asymmetry.

So, the finding in Chapter 3 that expert-adjusted forecasts often exceed model-based forecasts, sometimes called over-optimism, could also be assigned to the notion that experts have loss functions other than the squared loss function. And when forecasts are evaluated it is better to use accuracy criteria that are not based on the usual RMSPE-type criteria, as these assume symmetric error loss. So it could be that the findings in Chapter 4 that expert-adjusted forecasts are not much more accurate can be attributed to the criterion that is used to evaluate the forecasts.

However, the view in this monograph is that it is unlikely that experts adjusting model-based forecasts have explicitly incorporated alternative loss functions. The reason is that this is a rather difficult exercise to carry out, certainly on a regular basis dealing with many products. In fact, the reason why the squared error loss function is so popular is that the forecast is the conditional expectation, which is easy to compute, even manually. And, as Franses, Legerstee and Paap (2011) show, the forecast expressions corresponding with alternative loss functions are not at all straightforward to implement.

At the same time, suppose the experts really do have such alternative loss functions; one strategy to make them downplay their wish to modify model-based forecasts could be to instruct them that there is in fact no need to modify model forecasts when under-prediction is felt to be worse than over-prediction. In fact, one should try to convince them that the loss function for forecast creation is another loss function that is associated with managerial actions involving the size of the stock of products. Indeed, suppose a model-based forecast equals 1,000 units, then a manager (expert) can always decide to order 1,100 units so that out-of-stock conditions are less likely, and there is no need to quote an alternative forecast at all. In a similar vein, macroeconomic forecasters may know that revisions of macroeconomic variables like GDP are also usually upwards, and this knowledge can be implemented in discussions about forecasts. The model may give a 1.5 per cent growth, but in the public announcement it could be stated that such a 1.5 per cent may well turn out to be 2 per cent in a year's time. In the terminology of Chapter 2, one may try to convince the expert to stick to the Expert-Adjusted Forecast = Model Forecast + Adjustment rule, while at the same time, say, expert action (or communication, or policy) can be different from the expert-adjusted forecast (when adjustment is really necessary) or the model forecast.

Does it help to provide experts with feedback?

Lawrence *et al.* (2006) provide a review of the literature on judgemental forecasting up to 2006, and these authors discuss feedback and judgemental adjustments. In general, there is a distinction between outcome feedback, performance feedback and cognitive process feedback. Outcome feedback provides the expert with the realizations of the variable that they aim to forecast. This feedback is quite common as forecasters are usually able to observe past data, although it can occur that macroeconomic forecasters may have to wait a few years for the final data for their national accounts variables to be released. Lawrence *et al.* (2006) argue that outcome feedback is usually the least effective. In fact, Goodwin and Fildes (1999: 41) and Lawrence *et al.* (2006: 507) claim that forecasters seem unable to filter the noise component from the realized values and thereby face difficulties assessing systematic inadequacy in their forecasts, if there is any.

Second, performance feedback provides the forecaster with information on forecast accuracy with statistics such as the RMSPE. Basing their work on a laboratory experiment, Remus, O'Connor and Griggs (1996) are not able to report any evidence that performance feedback improves forecasting practices. On the other hand, Bolger and Önkal-Atay (2004) and Stone and Opel (2000) do find that performance feedback improves judgemental interval predictions and probability forecasts, instead of the point forecasts that are analysed in this monograph. Even though two of the principles in *The Principles of Forecasting* (Armstrong, 2001; Armstrong and Pagell, 2003) suggest that forecasting methods should be evaluated on their past performance and feedback on forecasts should be incorporated, Fildes *et al.* (2009) and Gönül, Önkal and Goodwin (2009) report that these principles are not often followed in practice. Recently, Athanasopoulos and Hyndman (2011) studied feedback not in a laboratory experiment but in an online forecasting competition. These two authors found that performance feedback significantly improves forecasting accuracy. Hence, it seems that the available evidence is not conclusive.

Third, cognitive process feedback gives the forecaster information on his or her own forecasting practices. This can include how the forecaster reacts to certain cues. Remus, O'Connor and Griggs (1996) report no evidence on the usefulness of cognitive process feedback and this confirms the results in Balzer *et al.* (1992) concerning probability forecasts.

Finally, an alternative type of feedback is called task properties feedback and it provides the forecaster with statistical information on the variable to be forecast such as data characteristics or statistical model forecasts. Some may argue that this cannot be considered to be true feedback as it is provided before (and not after) the expert-adjusted forecast is delivered, and also it is not feedback on the performance of the forecaster; see Björkman (1972). Interestingly, task properties feedback has received most attention in research on feedback on judgemental forecasting; see Sanders (1992), Remus, O'Connor and Griggs (1996), Welch, Bretschneider and Rohrbaugh (1998) and Goodwin and Fildes

(1999). It is found to improve forecast accuracy and in fact it is considered to be the most effective form of feedback (Lawrence *et al.* 2006). Another component of task properties feedback could be a more detailed explanation of the properties of the model. An example of useful information might be that models like the standard linear regression model assume symmetric errors, and this already suggests that more upward than downward adjustment would in principle not be correct. Furthermore, when recursive estimation methods are used, the effect of recent exceptional observations is already incorporated in the updated model forecast.

Legerstee and Franses (2014) consider a natural experiment based on the SKU-level sales data from Organon. Chapter 3 has already found that experts create final forecasts that deviate too much from the statistical model forecasts. Also, Chapter 4 reported that when the difference between the two forecasts increases, forecast accuracy decreases. The natural experiment in Legerstee and Franses (2014) was made possible by the fact that in August and September 2007 the Organon experts received feedback though a presentation at their headquarters' office. They received three kinds of feedback. First, they received cognitive process feedback, as statistics were presented on experts' behaviour when adjusting the statistical model forecasts. Second, they received performance feedback in the form of accuracy measures concerning their past expert-adjusted forecasts. Third, they received more detailed information and further explanation on the statistical models that were used to create the forecasts. Legerstee and Franses (2014) analysed the dataset with forecasts for the period September 2006 to September 2007 and compared it with the data from October 2007 to December 2007. Due to data limitations, as not all experts were present at the training, only twenty-one experts are involved in their analysis.

The findings in Legerstee and Franses (2014) are quite striking. The average size of the adjustments drops by about 80 per cent (see 2014: Table I), and the number of downward adjustments increases, thereby bringing more balance in the signs of adjustments. Their Table III shows a significant decline in very large and positive adjustments.

The subsequent tables in their study show that forecast accuracy significantly improves after feedback. The key conclusion of their study is that 'smaller adjustment in an absolute sense and more balance between the amount of positive and negative adjustments clearly increases forecast accuracy' (2014: 78). At the same time, their conclusion is that cognitive process feedback, performance feedback and extra information on the statistical model make experts create adjustments that lead to higher forecast accuracy.

In sum, informing experts that there is no need to have alternative loss functions and in particular to provide them with feedback on their behaviour may lead to changes in experts' adjustment behaviour to the benefit of forecast accuracy.

IMPROVING MODEL FORECASTS

Some of the cases examined in Chapters 3 and 4 involved model-based forecasts that were biased. Such a model forecast bias increases the inclination of experts to manipulate forecasts, sometimes to the good, but sometimes not. Such biased model forecasts could occur in Mathews and Diamantopoulos (1989) for Holt–Winters forecasting schemes, but apparently the CPB model could also deliver biased forecasts. This might occur because not all estimated parameters are updated each time the model is used to generate forecasts, and also because many parameters are somehow fixed, based on the domain-specific knowledge of the model-builders involved. For the CPB forecasts the involvement of the experts may lead to a smaller tendency to manipulate model forecasts, simply because the experts and the model-builders are grouped in similar teams. Consequently, Chapter 3 showed that for the CPB case the size of the differences between expert-adjusted forecasts and model forecasts was much smaller than those differences for the SKU sales forecasts.

Including experts' insights in the model: does it help?

Concerning the SKU sales forecasts, one may wonder whether perhaps the model forecasts can be improved by adding explanatory variables to the model, thereby possibly reducing the size of the experts' adjustment. As already mentioned, many FSS include just lagged sales data, while perhaps other data could also be useful. One might then think of past model-based forecast errors, past expert-adjusted forecast errors, and even past variation (volatility) in these variables. At the same time, experts could have had sensible and relevant insights in the past, which they incorporated into their modified forecasts. If these insights were useful, then it might also make sense to include past experts' knowledge in the statistical model.

This line of thought is pursued in Franses and Legerstee (2013), who generate a set of new model forecasts, which they then compare with the original model forecasts and the associated expert-adjusted forecasts. In fact, they consider the following regression model for the sales data, that is,

$$y_t = \mu + \rho_1 y_{t-1} + \rho_2 y_{t-2} + \beta_1 \hat{y}^E_{t|t-1} + \beta_2 (\hat{y}^E_{t|t-1} - \hat{y}_{t|t-1}) + u_t.$$
(5.5)

Note that the first part of the model involves the two lagged sales series, and that these are also included in the original forecasting models, but rarely in the form of this particular regression model. In fact, the original Organon model forecasts allow for up to twelve lags. The model in (5.5) extends the regression model containing two lags with lagged expert-adjusted forecasts and with lagged differences between expert-adjusted forecasts and model forecasts. Of course, many other variants are possible, but (5.5) already provides some useful insights.

Upon comparing these new model forecasts with the associated and available expert-adjusted forecasts, Franses and Legerstee (2013) find that when the new model performs better in terms of accuracy it is much better in an absolute sense than when the new model forecasts perform worse. They also find that there are various cases where the model forecasts benefit from including past experts-based information. In fact, as a general guideline the authors recommend that when past expert-adjusted forecasts and past model-based forecasts are not very accurate, then it is better to use versions of (5.5) for the statistical model forecasts. They even go as far as recommending always including past expertise, thus modifying the statistical algorithms used. This is because they find that 'when past judgment was not necessary, the harm is relatively small' (Franses and Legerstee, 2013: 86).

COMBINING FORECASTS

The third person involved in the discussion in this book is of course the analyst. There is the model-builder who creates the model forecasts, the expert who manipulates the model forecast, and the analyst who has to evaluate the relative merits of the two sets of forecasts. When such an analyst is equivalent to an end-user, who has the model forecast and the expert-adjusted forecast, the analyst may also decide to combine the two forecasts to see if a combination leads to better forecasts. Some hints have already been presented in Chapter 4, but a few more details of the SKU-level sales forecasts and the CPB forecasts can be illuminating.

Combining expert-adjusted forecasts with model forecasts

Again using the Organon database, and inspired by the first tentative results in Franses and Legerstee (2010) that the 50 per cent/50 per cent rule is perhaps better, many more results on combinations are presented in Franses and Legerstee (2011b). For thirty-seven experts and twelve forecast horizons, these authors consider the linear combinations

$$(1 - \alpha)\hat{y}_{t|t-h}^{E} + \alpha\hat{y}_{t|t-h}. \tag{5.6}$$

The performance of these combined forecasts is evaluated against the realizations again using the RMSPE criterion. The authors plug in for α the values 0, 0.05, 0.10, ..., 0.95, and 1. This amounts to twenty-one values for α. Of the 444 cases (thirty-seven experts and twelve horizons), the authors report that in only 4.73 per cent of the cases does the value of $\alpha = 0$ minimize the RMSPE criterion. This means that it rarely occurs that only the expert-adjusted forecasts have the highest accuracy relative to other combinations of expert forecasts and model forecasts. The same holds for the model forecasts only, as in only 5.86 per cent of the cases is it found that $\alpha = 1$ is best. In the remaining 89.41 per cent of the cases the combined forecast as in (5.6), with α in between 0 and 1, performs best. Franses and Legerstee (2011b) also compute per forecast horizon the average α value across the thirty-seven experts and this appears to range between 0.49 and 0.55. Hence, the 50 per cent/50 per cent rule, on average for all horizons, seems to work in the case of the Organon data.

In the ideal situation that

$$\hat{y}_{t|t-1}^{E} = \hat{y}_{t|t-1} + A_{t|t-1}, \tag{5.7}$$

meaning that Expert-Adjusted forecasts = Model Forecasts (with weight 1) + Adjustment, the 50 per cent/50 per cent rule would mean that an optimal combined forecast is

$$0.5\hat{y}_{t|t-1}^{E} + 0.5\hat{y}_{t|t-1} = \hat{y}_{t|t-1} + 0.5A_{t|t-1}. \tag{5.8}$$

In the apparently non-optimal situation described in Chapter 4, the situation for the Organon forecasts is, on average,

$$\beta\hat{y}_{t|t-1} + \gamma(\hat{y}_{t|t-1}^{E} - \lambda\hat{y}_{t|t-1}) \tag{5.9}$$

where λ is about 0.4, and β is approximately equal to γ. It is easily seen that (5.9) becomes

$$0.6\beta\hat{y}_{t|t-1} + \beta\hat{y}_{t|t-1}^{E} \tag{5.10}$$

giving relatively more weight to the expert-adjusted forecast – more than 50 per cent/50 per cent. Putting this balance back to 50 per cent/ 50 per cent, as done above in (5.8), shows that forecast gain can be acquired. It is unclear whether the 50 per cent/50 per cent rule is always useful, but the most prominent finding in Franses and Legerstee (2011b) is that the combined forecasts almost always beat their constituent components.

What makes the average forecast work?

Turning to the notion that expert-adjusted forecasts can be approximated by an analyst using publicly available data, one may wonder what it is that makes a combined and average forecast perform better. One way to approach this issue is to assume that an expert creates his or her own model, and adds some (un-replicable) intuition to it, as follows,

$$\hat{y}^E_{t|t-1} = \kappa \hat{y}_{t|t-1} + W_{t-1}\delta + I^*_{t|t-1} \qquad (5.11)$$

where W_{t-1} summarizes all kinds of variables that are not in the model forecast and where $I^*_{t|t-1}$ denotes genuine intuition, which cannot be observed by an analyst. The variables in W_{t-1} can be lagged model forecast errors, lagged expert forecast errors, measures of past volatility of the data, and so on. Basically, the linear combination of the forecasts can then be viewed as

$$(1 - \alpha)\hat{y}^*_{t|t-1} + \alpha \hat{y}_{t|t-1} \qquad (5.12)$$

where $\hat{y}^*_{t|t-1}$ is the model forecast that the expert uses, and which can be replicated approximately by the analyst, and this is the fit of (5.11). Again using the Organon data, Franses (2011b) documents that the linear combination, which can be constructed by the analyst, that is,

$$0.5\hat{y}^*_{t|t-1} + 0.5\hat{y}_{t|t-1} \qquad (5.13)$$

is about as equally good as

$$0.5\hat{y}^E_{t|t-1} + 0.5\hat{y}_{t|t-1}. \qquad (5.14)$$

In other words, the more expert-adjusted forecasts are replicable and are apparently based on various explanatory variables, which are mainly variables that were not included in the FSS that created the model forecasts, the better the linearly combined forecasts. In turn, this again suggests that the model forecasts can be improved by including various additional variables, which was already indicated earlier in this chapter.

Combined forecasts for the CPB

The annual CPB forecasts as they are presented in Kranendonk, de Jong and Verbruggen (2009) can also be combined with alternative forecasts created by an analyst. Suppose that this analyst only uses a real-time data-based univariate time series model; see Franses (2013b) for more details. Combining the latter forecasts with the CPB forecasts also leads to improvement (see Table 5.1). Hence, even combining the expert-based CPB forecasts with the forecasts from simple time series models helps to improve forecast accuracy by 5.8 per cent, on average.

Table 5.1: *Performance of CPB forecasts and equally weighted combined forecasts (from simple time series models) in terms of RMSPE*

Variable	CPB	Equal weights	Percentage improvement
GDP	1.556	1.522	–2.2%
World trade (V)	3.328	3.069	–7.8%
World trade (P)	5.366	5.151	–4.0%
Imports (P)	7.146	7.249	1.4%
Market wages	1.366	1.152	–15.7%
CPI	0.840	0.875	4.2%
Exports (P)	6.195	6.270	1.2%
GDP deflator	1.042	1.029	–1.2%
Exports (V)	4.508	3.931	–12.8%
Imports (V)	4.128	3.936	–4.7%
Consumption (V)	1.718	1.305	–24.1%
Investments (V)	5.139	5.558	8.2%
Employment	0.987	0.807	–18.2%
Average			–5.8%

V = volume

P = price

Source: Table 6 of Franses (2013b). Percentage improvement is computed as 100 times RMSPE equal weights minus RMSPE CPB divided by RMSPE CPB.

CONCLUSION

This chapter has presented various strategies to potentially improve the accuracy of forecasts, where these forecasts can be the model-based forecasts as well as the expert-adjusted forecasts. At the same time it has been demonstrated that combined forecasts also seem to improve on each of these two sets of forecasts.

Concerning expert-adjusted forecasts, it was shown that when these forecasts perform less well, it was due to the fact that the experts adjust more than necessary and that their forecasts can be approximated to a lesser extent by a replicable model created by an analyst. So the closer the expert sticks to his or her own replicable model, with variables other than in the available model, the better the combination.

6   Conclusion, limitations and implications

This book has analysed the situation in which an expert receives a model-based forecast that he or she may decide to modify, driven by domain-specific knowledge but perhaps also by unobservable and non-replicable intuition. In various chapters it was assumed that an analyst had access to both forecasts, while in Chapters 3 and 5 the situation was also considered where an analyst would only observe the expert-adjusted forecasts and not the model that may have been used by the expert. In that case, the analyst could revert to his or her own econometric skills to create model-based forecasts in order to be able to assess the accuracy and merits of the expert-adjusted forecasts.

This chapter first summarizes the main findings in this book, based on the empirical evidence reported in the relevant literature. Then the limitations are discussed, together with some potential implications for model-builders, experts and analysts. Next, it will provide an outlook for future research, which is mainly driven by the observation that most available forecasts in macroeconomics and business are not created only by an econometric model and many if not all of these forecasts amount to expert-adjusted forecasts.

CONCLUSION

Analysing various recent and also some thirty-year-old studies on expert-adjusted forecasts, and based on a variety of recently available databases, one of the most prominent insights from this book is that final forecasts are rarely based on pure econometric models. Forecasts for a range of macroeconomic variables in various countries (both thirty years ago and today) for SKU-level sales for a range of products across various companies and industries, and for airline revenues, all seem to be only partly based on the outcome of econometric models or statistical algorithms. At the same time, when experts have such forecasts from formal models at their disposal, we learn that they almost always seem to deviate from these model-based forecasts. This holds true for large-scale macroeconomic models and for simple extrapolation schemes, and it seems independent of the proven and reported quality of these models. This can be observed for the cases where model-based forecasts are explicitly available, and it also holds for the situations where an analyst (and thus the expert too) can create an approximate model forecast using publicly available data.

Hence, it seems fair to conclude that most forecasts are an interaction between a model and an expert. As Chapter 2 indicated, this is not necessarily bad practice, as there are econometric arguments why modified forecasts are useful and can also be more accurate. In practice, this means that many forecasts that an analyst has to evaluate are somehow a weighted sum of a model forecast and an adjustment, where it may be unknown where the adjustment comes from. An adjustment may originate from an expert's own model but it may also reflect non-replicable intuition. So, generally, it is the case that

$$\text{Expert-Adjusted Forecast} = \alpha \text{ Model Forecast} + \text{Adjustment}.$$

Usually it is unknown what the value of α is and what the size of that added term is, and frequently the model forecast is also not available to the analyst. In Chapter 2 it was argued that an optimal situation appears when $\alpha = 1$, with the adjustment orthogonal to the model forecast, and the adjustment being unpredictable, but in practice extreme cases with $\alpha = 0$ may also occur. Chapter 2 also stated that it can be very useful if an expert modifies a model-based forecast. Exceptional observations may occur at the forecast origin, or experts may foresee exceptional observations in the near future, based on their domain-specific knowledge. There is, however, no reason why experts should almost always modify model forecasts, nor why they should mainly adjust upwards or mainly downwards. It appears that only when the adjustment part is relevant and the value of α is close to 1, might the modified forecast be reliable and lead to more accuracy.

Drawing on a range of case studies and large databases, Chapter 3 demonstrated that non-zero expert adjustment of model-based forecasts is more the rule than the exception. Even more so, it seems that, on average, experts favour adjusting upwards more than downwards, and this does not match the ideal situation outlined in Chapter 2. Chapter 4 showed that when experts' adjusted forecasts substantially deviate from model forecasts, either the actual ones or the approximated ones, then forecast accuracy deteriorates. Small and rare adjustments seem to be most associated with more accuracy.

Chapter 5 reviewed a few ways of improving both the expert-adjusted forecasts, and the model-based forecasts. Feedback was found to make a difference, and the combination of expert forecasts and model forecasts was also found to yield substantial improvement.

LIMITATIONS

The analysis in this book has various limitations. First, the econometric analysis in Chapter 2 was based on a few important assumptions. The econometric model should be correctly specified, and there should be no obvious (to the expert) omitted variables. Also, the parameters should be estimated consistently and the resulting forecasts should be unbiased. When properly carried out, such econometric models usually deliver unbiased forecasts, but there are various reasons why biases may occur. Modellers may not update parameter estimates each time, and measurement errors in explanatory variables may also lead to bias. In macroeconomics, the notion that data are updated for various years in a row also increases the probability of having biased forecasts.

Another important assumption in Chapter 2 was that the experts who receive the model forecasts believe that these forecasts are unbiased. This is a strong assumption, as sometimes the model forecasts are based on simple extrapolation schemes, which do not contain all kinds of domain-specific variables. At the same time, omitted variables do not always lead to biased forecasts.

A further limitation of this book is that the focus has been on point forecasts. The main reason for that is data availability. But other forecasts are relevant too, and one can then think of interval forecasts and probability forecasts.

Finally, a serious limitation of the analysis presented here is that it is unclear what experts do. There is some anecdotal evidence and there are some surveys, but detailed logbooks with quotes and comments on the reasons why experts adjust forecasts are not available. This seriously hampers the analysis, as all analysts can do is try to approximate what experts might have done. The first equation in this book is therefore a linear equation, mainly because the subsequent analysis is then simple. There are no available indications that experts multiply model forecasts with their own insights. At the same time, there is no specific information on the actual loss functions of experts. With subtle statistical analysis, one could get an impression of what the loss function could have been, but this is also only an approximation.

Finally, as already mentioned in the first chapter, it is usually unknown whether the experts work alone or in teams. When they do the latter, all sorts of additional biases can appear, where group-think and group pressure can lead to alternatively formulated adjusted forecasts.

IMPLICATIONS

Notwithstanding the limitations, the results summarized in this monograph do seem to lead to some implications for model-builders, experts and analysts. These could be useful in the future when they create, adjust or evaluate forecasts.

Econometric model-builders and those who use statistical algorithms to create model-based forecasts should perhaps provide more information on how the model forecasts were created; in other words, which variables were included, how were the parameters estimated, how were the forecasts created, and based on which available information? Also, they should aim to create unbiased forecasts, and when their model forecasts are not unbiased, they should be able to inform the experts what the origins of those biases are. At the same time, when forecasts are not biased, as was demonstrated for the Organon data, model-builders should inform the experts about this absence of bias. Finally, past adjustment by experts turned out to be a potentially useful inclusion in econometric models, so perhaps more information from experts can be explicitly incorporated into econometric models.

As has been demonstrated, experts have too strong a tendency to modify model-based forecasts, wherever these model forecasts come from. It would be helpful if the experts paid more attention to understanding where the model forecasts came from and how they were created. At the same time, they should learn that persistent adjustment cannot possibly be the best strategy. And, most importantly, the experts should provide documentation on why and how they decided to modify model forecasts. Finally, experts should become more aware that forecasts and managerial decisions are two different aspects. Managerial decisions can always deviate. If management so requires, one can always do something from what the forecasts imply, and there is then no reason to modify the forecasts.

An implication for analysts is that they should pay more attention to how the experts actually created their forecasts. More knowledge on this would facilitate the analysis of the accuracy of the forecasts and could also suggest future modifications to the model. Also, as was discussed in Chapter 5, feedback to experts and model-builders can lead to different and sometimes more useful expert behaviour. A further implication for analysts is that there is quite a lot more research to be carried out, as most currently used tools to evaluate forecasts almost invariably assume that the forecasts originate from an econometric model. When an expert has modified the forecast, matters become very different.

FUTURE RESEARCH

The notion that many available forecasts are the concerted outcome of models and adjustment has an impact on various other issues around forecasts, such as the evaluation of forecast accuracy, the computation of forecast intervals, and the analysis of forecast updates.

Evaluating forecasts

When most publicly available forecasts – for example those of the OECD, the World Bank, the IMF, and many others – are potentially the concerted effort of an econometric model and an expert's touch, where the touch can have weight 1 and the model weight 0, then one may need to rethink the methods of evaluating and comparing these forecasts. Most current methods to test and compare predictive accuracy, like those based on (extensions of) the seminal work by Diebold and Mariano (1995), assume that the forecasts are unbiased and typically emerge from competing econometric models. Asymptotic theory is then reasonably straightforward. However, when forecasts turn out to be based on econometric models and intuition in an unknown way, then matters become different. Franses, McAleer and Legerstee (2014) recommend first creating approximate replicable forecasts for the forecasts under scrutiny, and then comparing them. Chang, Franses and McAleer (2011) apply some of these ideas to government forecasts in Taiwan and report that it is the additional expertise of the forecasters in the Taiwanese government that substantially reduces forecast errors, due to their expertise. But it is expected that more methods will be designed to formally and statistically evaluate and compare expert forecasts.

Similarly, future research will also have to address the uncertainty bounds around the expert forecasts. It is reasonably straightforward to compute confidence intervals for (not too large) econometric models. However, it seems that when available final forecasts are an unknown combination of model forecasts and adjustment, new methods of estimating confidence bounds will be needed. This would then allow for a proper diagnosis of the uncertainty around expert forecasts. Preferably, one would find that expert forecasts have smaller bounds, as proper adjustment takes away some of the uncertainty from the model, at least in the ideal econometric situation. For the CPB variables, Franses (2013b) reports that the uncertainty in the expert forecasts is about equal to the uncertainty implied from univariate time series models, and thus some improvement is to be gained there.

Fixed-event forecast revisions

Finally, assuming that available forecasts are the concerted outcome of the input from an econometric model and from adjustment can also lead to understanding recent puzzling empirical evidence in the literature. An interesting recent account of this is provided in Chang *et al.* (2013), where the authors address an anomaly for so-called forecast updates. Consider a forecast given at origin $t - h$ for an event at the fixed target date t as $F_{t|t-h}$, where $h = 1, \ldots, H$. For each event t, there are H forecasts, that is, a one-step-ahead forecast to an H-steps-ahead forecast. A forecast revision is usually defined by $F_{t|t-h} - F_{t|t-(h+1)}$. A method often used to examine such forecast revisions involves an auxiliary regression of the form

$$F_{t|t-h} - F_{t|t-(h+1)} = \alpha + \beta\big(F_{t|t-(h+1)} - F_{t|t-(h+2)}\big) + \xi_{t,h}, \qquad (6.1)$$

where the parameter β is of key interest, where h runs from 1 to H, and where the sample size is H. This regression, which is advocated in Nordhaus (1987), is typically used to test so-called weak-form efficiency, which predicts that the correlation between subsequent forecast revisions is zero. Interestingly, and as reviewed in Chang *et al.* (2013), this null hypothesis is almost invariably rejected in practice. This cannot be the case when pure econometric models are used. However, when the authors allow that forecasts are partly based on an econometric model and partly on adjustment, then values of β can be associated with various time series properties of adjustment. Depending on these properties, β can have positive or negative values. Perhaps more such apparently contradictory results for economic forecasts can be explained to some extent by the adoption of the concept

Expert-Adjusted Forecast = α Model Forecast + Adjustment.

Future research will hopefully lead to these and many more insights.

Data appendix

Table A1: *Real GDP data the Netherlands used in Chapter 2. These were retrieved from Statistics Netherlands in November 2007. The measurement unit is millions of euros.*

	Quarter			
Year	Q1	Q2	Q3	Q4
1988	69350	70921	68045	72999
1989	72265	74340	70904	76242
1990	75309	77013	73900	79816
1991	76924	79356	75714	81511
1992	79683	80409	76771	81988
1993	79841	81625	78435	82958
1994	81582	84004	80745	86086
1995	84657	86510	83178	88431
1996	86539	89879	86365	91667
1997	89943	93688	89985	95997
1998	94533	97218	93005	99362
1999	98335	101369	97275	105131
2000	103402	105895	100729	107934
2001	105826	108443	102553	109187
2002	105615	108529	103105	109086
2003	106499	108278	103107	109883
2004	108188	110518	105764	112866
2005	108750	112308	107844	115040
2006	112534	115738	110912	118098
2007	115306	118792	115506	

Table A2: *Data on three characteristics of the Organon experts. Age and position are measured in years. Gender is a 1/0 dummy variable where 1 denotes females. When two or more experts are responsible for the forecasting task, the data are averaged.*

Country	Age	Position	Gender
1	55	10	0
2	30	5	0
3	40	5	0
4	45	10	0.5
5	45	5	1
6	30	2	0
7	60	15	1
8	30	3	1
9	30	4	0.5
10	35	5	1
11	25	2	1
12	35	5	1
13	35	5	1
14	55	15	1
15	45	10	0
16	35	5	0
17	55	20	1
18	30	10	0
19	50	15	0
20	35	10	0
21	40	1	1
22	50	20	0
23	37.5	15	0
24	40	15	1
25	35	5	1
26	35	3	0
27	47.5	17.5	0
28	32.5	7.5	0
29	40	3	1
30	45	10	0
31	60	20	0
32	20	10	1
33	45	7	0
34	30	1	1
35	30	5	0
36	30	5	1
37	45	5	1
Average	39.5	8.4	0.486

Table A3: *Data for the Organon experts concerning their one-step-ahead forecasts. Size and Sign are defined as in (3.8) and (3.9), respectively, whereas Products represents the number of products for which the experts make forecasts as a measure of experience. The underlined observation is an outlier.*

Country	Size	Sign	Products
1	0.591	0.780	305
2	1.012	0.591	472
3	0.979	0.529	1004
4	0.342	0.612	922
5	0.648	0.610	1227
6	0.243	0.450	100
7	8.712	0.556	514
8	1.115	0.678	884
9	0.200	0.636	176
10	2.317	0.653	372
11	0.409	0.530	864
12	0.392	0.582	928
13	0.452	0.620	300
14	0.351	0.624	1200
15	1.014	0.479	1602
16	0.264	0.580	2182
17	1.134	0.597	761
18	0.340	0.302	943
19	1.023	0.623	886
20	0.490	0.558	283
21	0.782	0.556	665
22	1.467	0.745	298
23	0.259	0.588	1445
24	0.390	0.402	1155
25	0.993	0.425	412
26	0.477	0.531	638
27	0.793	0.491	922
28	0.328	0.561	508
29	0.239	0.506	1060
30	0.307	0.580	1306
31	0.222	0.596	1412
32	1.409	0.278	352
33	0.566	0.697	241
34	5.630	0.539	1921
35	0.961	0.592	265
36	1.759	0.575	779
37	1.267	0.601	529

Table A.4: *Data for the Organon experts concerning their six-steps-ahead forecasts. Size and Sign are defined as in (3.8) and (3.9), respectively, whereas Products represents the number of products for which the experts make forecasts as a measure of experience.*

Country	Size	Sign	Products
1	0.374	0.775	240
2	1.273	0.583	379
3	0.993	0.441	780
4	0.428	0.568	725
5	0.548	0.579	952
6	0.315	0.488	800
7	24.27	0.541	390
8	1.301	0.723	704
9	0.240	0.652	138
10	2.116	0.695	279
11	0.510	0.454	678
12	0.490	0.573	722
13	0.346	0.589	236
14	0.508	0.560	952
15	1.738	0.476	1278
16	0.604	0.539	1730
17	1.016	0.599	599
18	0.310	0.237	746
19	0.709	0.612	704
20	1.513	0.610	223
21	1.278	0.537	520
22	1.899	0.794	233
23	0.340	0.614	1147
24	0.237	0.407	919
25	2.466	0.329	304
26	0.317	0.562	500
27	0.959	0.464	716
28	0.378	0.610	397
29	0.546	0.464	845
30	0.404	0.531	1031
31	0.371	0.591	1120
32	1.763	0.240	246
33	0.605	0.649	188
34	0.616	0.545	1528
35	0.804	0.521	165
36	1.774	0.499	605
37	0.962	0.581	420

References

Armstrong, J. S. (2001), Combining forecasts, in J. S. Armstrong (ed.), *The Principles of Forecasting: A Handbook for Researchers and Practitioners*, Norwell, MA: Kluwer.

Armstrong, J. S. and R. Pagell (2003), The ombudsman: Reaping benefits from management research: Lessons from the forecasting principles project, *Interfaces*, **33**, 91–7.

Athanasopoulos, G. and R. J. Hyndman (2011), The value of feedback in forecasting competitions, *International Journal of Forecasting*, **27**, 845–9.

Auster, P. (2012) *Winter Journal*, London: Picador.

Balzer, W. K., L. M. Sulsky, L. B. Hammer and K. E. Sumner (1992), Task information, cognitive information, or functional validity information: Which components of cognitive feedback affect performance?, *Organizational Behavior and Human Decision Processes*, **53**, 35–54.

Barber, B. and T. Odean (2001), Boys will be boys: Gender, overconfidence, and common stock investment, *Quarterly Journal of Economics*, **116**, 261–92.

Belsley, D. A. (1988), Modeling and forecasting reliability, *International Journal of Forecasting*, **4**, 427–47.

Beyer, S. and E. Bowden (1997), Gender differences in self-perceptions: Convergent evidence from three measures of accuracy and bias, *Personality and Social Psychology Bulletin*, **23**, 157–72.

Blattberg, R. C. and S. J. Hoch (1990), Database models and managerial intuition: 50% model + 50% manager, *Management Science*, **36**, 887–99.

Björkman, M. (1972), Feedforward and feedback as determiners of knowledge and policy-notes on a neglected issue, *Scandinavian Journal of Psychology*, **13**, 152–8.

Bolger, F. and D. Önkal-Atay (2004), The effects of feedback on judgmental interval predictions, *International Journal of Forecasting*, **20**, 29–39.

Boulaksil, Y. and P. H. Franses (2009), Experts' stated behavior, *Interfaces*, **39**, 168–71.

Bunn, D. W. (1992), Synthesis of expert judgment and statistical forecasting models or decision support, in G. Wright and F. Bolger (eds.), *Expertise and Decision Support*, New York: Plenum, 251–68.

Bunn, D. W. and A. A. Salo (1996), Adjustment of forecasts with model consistent expectations, *International Journal of Forecasting*, **12**, 163–70.

Camerer, Colin F. (1989), Does the basketball market believe in the 'hot hand'?, *American Economic Review*, **74**, 1257–61.

Chen, C. and L.-M. Liu (1993), Joint estimation of model parameters and outlier effects in time series, *Journal of the American Statistical Association*, **88**, 284–97.

Chevillon, G. (2007), Direct multi-step estimation and forecasting, *Journal of Economic Surveys*, **21**, 746–85.

Chang, C.-L., P. H. Franses and M. McAleer (2011), How accurate are government forecasts of economic fundamentals? The case of Taiwan, *International Journal of Forecasting*, **27**, 1066–75.

Chang, C.-L., B. de Bruijn, P. H. Franses and M. McAleer (2013), Analyzing fixed-event forecast revisions, *International Journal of Forecasting*, **29**, 622–7.

Christoffersen, P. and F. X. Diebold (1996), Further results on forecasting and model selection under asymmetric loss, *Journal of Applied Econometrics*, **11**, 561–71.

(1997), Optimal prediction under asymmetric loss, *Econometric Theory*, **13**, 808–17.

Clark, T. E. and M. W. McCracken (2001), Tests of equal forecast accuracy and encompassing for nested models, *Journal of Econometrics*, **105**, 85–110.

(2005), Evaluating direct multi-step forecasts, *Econometric Reviews*, **24**, 369–404.

CPB (1992), *FKSEC, A Macro-econometric Model for the Netherlands*, Leiden: Stenfert Kroese.

CPB (2003), SAFE, A quarterly model of the Dutch economy for short-term analyses, CPB Document 42.

Croson, R. and U. Gneezy (2009), Gender differences in preferences, *Journal of Economic Literature*, **47**, 448–74.

(1979), The robust beauty of improper linear models in decision making, *American Psychologist*, **34**, 571–82.

De Bondt, W. F. M. and R. H. Thaler (1987), Further evidence on investor overreaction and stock market seasonality, *Journal of Finance*, **42**, 557–81.

De Bruijn, B. and P. H. Franses (2012), Managing sales forecasters, Tinbergen Institute Discussion Paper 12–131/III, Erasmus University Rotterdam.

Diamantopoulos, A. and B. P. Mathews (1989), Factors affecting the nature and effectiveness of subjective revision in sales forecasting: An empirical study, *Managerial and Decision Economics*, **10**, 51–9.

Diebold, F. X. and R. S. Mariano (1995), Comparing predictive accuracy, *Journal of Business and Economic Statistics*, **13**, 253–63.

Don, H. (2004), How econometric models help policy makers: theory and practice, CPB Discussion Paper 27, The Hague.

Don, H. and J. P. Verbruggen (2006), Models and methods for economic policy: 60 years of evolution at CPB, *Statistica Neerlandica*, **60**, 145–70.

Donihue, M. R. (1993), Evaluating the role judgment plays in forecast accuracy, *Journal of Forecasting*, **12**, 81–92.

Durham, G. R., M. G. Hertzel and J. S. Martin (2005), The market impact of trends and sequences in performance: New evidence, *Journal of Finance*, **60**, 2551–69.

Eckel, C. C. and P. J. Grossman (2008), Forecasting risk attitudes: An experimental study using actual and forecast gamble attitudes, *Journal of Economic Behavior and Organization*, **68**, 1–17.

Edmundson, R., M. Lawrence and M. O'Connor (1988), The use of non time series information in time series forecasting, *Journal of Forecasting*, **7**, 201–12.

Elliott, G., I. Komunjer and A. Timmermann (2005), Estimation and testing of forecast rationality under flexible loss, *Review of Economic Studies*, **72**, 1107–25.

Eriksson, K. and B. Simpson (2010), Emotional reactions to losing explain gender differences in entering a risky lottery, *Judgment and Decision Making*, **3**, 159–63.

Ferguson, T. (1967), *Mathematical Statistics: A Decision Theoretic Approach*, New York: Academic Press.

Fildes, R., and Goodwin, P. (2007), Good and bad judgment in forecasting: Lessons from four companies, *Foresight: The International Journal of Applied Forecasting*, **8**, 5–10.

Fildes, R., P. Goodwin, M. Lawrence and K. Nikolopoulos (2009), Effective forecasting and judgmental adjustments: An empirical evaluation and strategies for improvement in supply-chain planning, *International Journal of Forecasting*, **25**, 3–23.

Fischoff, B. (1988), Judgemental aspects of forecasting: Needs and possible trends, *International Journal of Forecasting*, **4**, 331–9.

Fox, A. J. (1972), Outliers in time series, *Journal of the Royal Statistical Society B*, **34**, 350–63.

Franses, P. H. (1998), *Time Series Models for Business and Economic Forecasting*, Cambridge University Press.

(2004), Do we think we make better forecasts than in the past?: A survey of academics, *Interfaces*, **34**, 466–8.

(2011a), Marketing and sales, in M. P. Clements and D. F. Hendry (eds.), *The Oxford Handbook on Economic Forecasting*, Oxford: Oxford University Press, ch. 25.

(2011b), Averaging model forecasts and expert forecasts: Why does it work?, *Interfaces*, **41**, 177–81.

(2013a) Improving judgmental adjustment of model-based Forecasts, *Mathematics and Computers in Simulation*, **93**, 1–8.

(2013b), Evaluating CPBs forecasts, Manuscript under revision for re-submission.

Franses, P. H., H. Kranendonk and D. Lanser (2011), One model and various experts: Evaluating Dutch macroeconomics forecasts, *International Journal of Forecasting*, **27**, 482–95.

Franses, P. H. and R. Legerstee (2009), Properties of expert adjustments on model-based SKU-level forecasts, *International Journal of Forecasting*, **25**, 35–47.

(2010), Do experts' adjustments on model-based SKU-level forecasts improve forecast quality? *Journal of Forecasting*, **29**, 331–40.

(2011a), Experts' adjustment to model-based SKU-level forecasts: Does the forecast horizon matter?, *Journal of the Operational Research Society*, **62**, 537–43.

(2011b), Combining SKU-level sales forecasts from models and experts, *Experts Systems with Applications*, **38**, 2365–70.

(2013), Do statistical forecasting models for SKU-level data benefit from including past expert knowledge?, *International Journal of Forecasting*, **29**, 80–7.

Franses, P. H., R. Legerstee and R. Paap (2011), Estimating loss functions of experts, Tinbergen Institute Discussion Paper 177/4, Erasmus School of Economics.

Franses, P. H., M. McAleer and R. Legerstee (2009), Expert opinion versus expertise in forecasting, *Statistica Neerlandica*, **63**, 334–46.

(2014), Evaluating macroeconomic forecasts: A concise review of some recent developments, *Journal of Economic Surveys*, **28**, 195–208.

Franses, P. H. and R. Paap (2002), Censored latent effects autoregression, with an application to US unemployment, *Journal of Applied Econometrics*, **17**, 347–66.

Glisky, E. L. (2007), Changes in cognitive function in human aging, in D. R. Riddle (ed.), *Brain Aging: Models, Methods, Mechanisms*, Boca Raton, FL: CRC Press, pp. 1–15.

Gönül, S., D. Önkal and P. Goodwin (2009), Expectations, use and judgmental adjustment of external financial and economic forecasts: An empirical investigation, *International Journal of Forecasting*, **28**, 19–37.

Gönül, M. S., D. Önkal and M. Lawrence (2006), The effects of structural characteristics of explanations on use of a DSS, *Decision Support Systems*, **42**, 1481–93.

Goodwin, P. (2000), Improving the voluntary integration of statistical forecasts and judgment, *International Journal of Forecasting*, **16**, 85–99.

Goodwin, P. and R. Fildes (1999), Judgmental forecasts of time series affected by special events: Does providing a statistical forecast improve accuracy?, *Journal of Behavioral Decision Making*, **12**, 37–53.

Granger, C. W. J. and M. J. Morris (1976), Time series modelling and interpretation, *Journal of the Royal Statistical Society* A, **139**, 246–57.

Granger, C. W. J. and P. Newbold (1986), *Forecasting Economic Time Series*, San Diego: Academic Press.

Gysler, M., J. B. Kruse and R. Schubert (2002), Ambiguity and gender differences in financial decision making: An experimental examination of competence and confidence effects, Unpublished working paper, Swiss Federal Institute of Technology.

Haitovsky, Y. And G. I. Treyz (1972), Forecasts with quarterly macroeconomic models, equation adjustments and benchmark predictions: the U.S. experience, *Review of Economics and Statistics*, **54**, 317–25.

Harvey, N (1995), Why are judgments less consistent in less predictable task situations? *Organizational Behavior and Human Decision Processes*, **63**, 247–63.

Heath, C. and A. Tversky (1991), Preference and belief: Ambiguity and competence in choice under uncertainty, *Journal of Risk and Uncertainty*, **4**, 5–28.

Howrey, E. P., L. R. Klein and M. D. McCarthy (1974), Notes on testing the predictive performance of econometric models, *International Economic Review*, **15**, 366–83.

Huss, W. R. (1986), Comparative analysis of company forecasts and advanced time-series techniques using annual electric utility energy sales data, *International Journal of Forecasting*, **1**, 217–39.

Hyndman, R. J. (2013), Forecasting without forecasters, Keynote lecture at the 2013 International Symposium on Forecasting, Seoul, Korea.

Kahneman, D. (2012), *Thinking, Fast and Slow*, London: Penguin.

Kliger, D. and O. Levy (2010), Overconfident investors and probability misjudgements, *Journal of Socio-Economics*, **39**, 24–9.

Kranendonk, H., J. de Jong and J. Verbruggen (2009), Accuracy of CPB forecasts 1971–2007, CPB Memorandum 178, Netherlands Bureau of Economic Policy Analysis.

Kranendonk, H. and J. Verbruggen (2007), SAFFIER, a multi-purpose model of the Dutch economy for short-term and medium-term analyses, CPB Document 144.

Lamont, O. A. (2002), Macroeconomic forecasts and microeconomic forecasters, *Journal of Economic Behavior and Organization*, **48**, 265–80.

Lawrence, M., P. Goodwin, M. O'Connor and D. Önkal (2006), Judgemental forecasting: A review of progress over the last 25 years, *International Journal of Forecasting*, **22**, 493–518.

Ledolter, J. (1989), The effect of additive outliers on the forecasts from ARIMA models, *International Journal of Forecasting*, **5**, 231–40.

Legerstee, R. and P. H. Franses (2007), Competence and confidence effects in experts' forecast adjustments, Econometric Institute Report 2007–8–30, Erasmus School of Economics.

    (2014), Do experts' SKU forecasts improve after feedback? *Journal of Forecasting*, **33**, 69–79.

Legerstee, R., P. H. Franses and R. Paap (2011), Do experts incorporate statistical model forecasts and should they?, Tinbergen Institute Discussion Paper, 11–154/4, Erasmus University, Rotterdam.

Makridakis, S. and M. Hibon (2000), The M3-competition: Results, conclusions and implications, *International Journal of Forecasting*, **16**, 451–76.

Mathews, B. and A. Diamantopoulos (1986), Managerial intervention in forecasting: An empirical investigation of forecast manipulation, *International Journal of Research in Marketing*, **3**, 3–10.

(1989), Judgmental revision of statistical forecasts: A longitudinal extension. *Journal of Forecasting*, **8**, 129–40.

McNees, R. K. (1990), The role of judgment in macroeconomic forecast accuracy, *International Journal of Forecasting*, **6**, 287–99.

Nordhaus, W. D. (1987), Forecasting efficiency: Concepts and application, *Review of Economics and Statistics*, **69**, 667–74.

Patton, A. J. and A. Timmermann (2007a), Properties of optimal forecasts under asymmetric loss and nonlinearity, *Journal of Econometrics*, **140**, 884–918.

(2007b), Testing forecast optimality under unknown loss, *Journal of the American Statistical Association*, **102**, 1172–84.

Powell, M. and D. Ansic (1997), Gender differences in risk behaviour in financial decision-making: An experimental analysis, *Journal of Economic Psychology*, **18**, 605–28.

Rabin, M. (2002), Inference by believers in the Law of Small Numbers, *Quarterly Journal of Economics*, **117**, 775–816.

Remus, W. E. M. J. O'Connor and K. Griggs (1996), Does feedback improve the accuracy of recurrent judgmental forecasts?, *Organizational Behavior and Human Decision Processes*, **66**, 22–30.

Sanders, N. R. (1992), Accuracy of judgmental forecasts: A comparison, *Omega*, **20**, 353–364.

(1997), The impact of task properties feedback on time series judgmental forecasting tasks, *Omega: The International Journal of Management Science*, **25**, 135–144.

Sanders, N. R. and L. Ritzman (2001), Judgemental adjustments of statistical forecasts, in J. S. Armstrong (ed.), *Principles of Forecasting*, New York: Kluwer.

Shanteau, J. (1992), The psychology of experts: An alternative view, in G. Wright and F. Bolger (eds.), *Expertise and Decision Support*, New York: Plenum, pp. 11–23.

Simon, H. A. (1992), What is an explanation of behavior?, *Psychological Science*, **3**, 150–61.

Singh-Manoux, A., M. Kivimaki, M. Glymour, A. Elbaz, C. Berr, K. B. Ebmeier, J. E. Ferrie and A. Dugravot (2012), Timing of onset of cognitive decline: Results from Whitehall II prospective cohort study, *British Medical Journal*, **344**, d7622.

Stekler, H. O. (2007), The future of macroeconomic forecasting: Understanding the forecasting process, *International Journal of Forecasting*, **23**, 237–48.

Stone, E. R. and Opel, R. B. (2000), Training to improve calibration and discrimination: The effects of performance and environmental feedback, *Organizational Behavior and Human Decision Processes*, **83**, 282–309.

Taleb, N. N. (2007), *The Black Swan: The Impact of the Highly Improbable*, New York: Random House.

Tetlock, P. E. (2005), *Expert Political Judgment: How Good is It? How Can We Know?*, Princeton University Press.

Timmermann, A. (2006), Forecast combinations, in G. Elliott, C. W. J. Granger and A. Timmermann (eds.), *Handbook of Economic Forecasting*, Vol. I, Amsterdam: Elsevier, pp. 135–96.

Tsay, R. S. (1988), Outliers, level shifts, and variance changes in time series, *Journal of Forecasting*, **7**, 1–20.

Turner, D. S. (1990), The role of judgment in macroeconomic forecasting, *Journal of Forecasting*, **9**, 319–45.

Tversky, A. and D. Kahneman (1971), Belief in the Law of Small Numbers, *Psychological Bulletin*, **76**, 105–10.

Varian, H. (1975), A Bayesian approach to real estate assessment, in S. Fienberg and A. Zellner (eds.), *Studies in Bayesian Econometrics and Statistics in Honor of Leonard J. Savage*, Amsterdam: North Holland, pp. 195–208.

Welch, E., S. Bretschneider and Rohrbaugh, J. (1998), Accuracy of judgmental extrapolation of time series data: Characteristics, causes, and remediation strategies for forecasting, *International Journal of Forecasting*, **14**, 95–110.

West, K. D. (1996), Asymptotic inference about predictive ability, *Econometrica*, **64**, 1067–84.

Willemain, T. R. (1989), Graphical adjustment of statistical forecasts, *International Journal of Forecasting*, **5**, 179–85.

Yaniv, I. and Kleinberger, E. (2000), Advice taking in decision making: egocentric discounting and reputation formation, *Organizational Behavior and Human Decision Processes*, **83**, 260–81.

Zellner, A. (1986), Bayesian estimation and prediction under asymmetric loss functions, *Journal of the American Statistical Association*, **81**, 446–51.

Index

Printed in the United States
By Bookmasters